Heirloom Flavor

Yesterday's Best-Tasting Vegetables, Fruits, and Herbs for Today's Cook

Doreen G. Howard

COOL SPRINGS PRESS

Growing Successful Gardeners™

Minneapolis, Minnesota

First Published in 2013 by Cool Springs Press, an imprint of the Quayside Publishing Group, 400 North First Avenue, Suite 400, Minneapolis, MN 55401 USA.

Cool Springs Press titles are also available at discounts in bulk quantity for industrial or sales-promotional use. For details write to Special Sales Manager at Cool Springs Press, 400 North First Avenue, Suite 400, Minneapolis, MN 55401 USA.

To find out more about our books, visit us online at www.coolspringspress.com.

Library of Congress Cataloging-in-Publication Data

Howard, Doreen.
  Heirloom flavor : yesterday's best-tasting vegetables, fruits, and herbs for today's cooks / Doreen G. Howard.
      p. cm.
  Includes bibliographical references and index.
  ISBN 978-1-59186-489-9 (softcover)
  1. Vegetables--Heirloom varieties. 2. Herbs--Heirloom varieties. 3. Fruit--Heirloom varieties. 4. Vegetable gardening. 5. Herb gardening. 6. Fruit-culture. I. Title. II. Title: Heirloom vegetables, herbs, & fruits.

  SB324.73.H68 2011
  635--dc22

                                    2010040120

President/CEO: Ken Fund
Design & Layout: Mark Ross & Chris Fayers

Printed in China
10 9 8 7 6 5 4 3 2 1

Acknowledgments

My deepest thanks and gratitude to the following people who shared their vast knowledge and experiences with me and with you, the reader: Dr. John Navazio, Mark Dwyer, Rotary Botanic Garden volunteers, Mayo Underwood, Alan Kapuler, Tom Wagner, Bill McDorman & Belle Starr, Deborah Phillips, Jim Long, Rose Marie Nichols-McGee, Rick Bayless, and Billie Brownell, whose editing talent and patience made this book possible.

Dedication

To Pete, who always makes me laugh.

Contents

The Return of Flavor

I'm an admitted foodie, always looking for new cuisines, dishes, and ingredients to explore. Porcini mushrooms and truffle oil enticed me to try the classic Italian dish polenta seasoned with both—something I initially found unappealing. Then I discovered that health-conscious chefs were using pureéd Rosa Bianca eggplant in place of cornmeal to make a lighter polenta. After sampling that sprightly, flavorful version at a four-star restaurant in Philadelphia, I couldn't find seeds for the Italian heirloom eggplant fast enough to plant that spring.

Growing my own lemongrass and Oriental basil introduced me into experimenting with Thai cuisine, and antique apples pushed me into creating tarts, sweet-savory roast pork toppings, and more. I'm not alone in my quest for the freshest and tastiest ingredients to fashion tantalizing, innovative foods. That's why farmers' markets are *packed* with shoppers, specialty grocers make large profits despite a tough economy, and why it can take *weeks* to get a reservation at restaurants specializing in creative cuisine.

Fresh ingredients—especially heirlooms—packed with flavors are the hallmark of great cuisine. Gourmet chefs are picky about the vegetables, fruits, and other foods that go into their mouth-watering creations. "You can't have great cuisine without using great local ingredients," maintains Rick Bayless, celebrity chef and chef-owner of the four-star Frontera Grill and Topolobampo Restaurant in Chicago. He features inspired dishes based on the heirlooms that are in season locally, like garlic-and-chile-marinated grilled Amish rock hens with charcoaled green onions, creamy poblano pepper soup with roasted sweet corn, and smoked ham hocks and carrots. "We seduce the customer first with flavor, and then we tell them about the ingredients and from where they come," Bayless says. As a result, heirlooms such as Russian Banana fingerling potatoes, Lettuce Leaf basil, and smoked Jalapeños have become mainstream. Like many chefs, Bayless has a kitchen garden (atop his restaurant), one at home, and an extensive light garden in his basement to grow heirloom specialties that make his world-class cuisine, brimming with layers of flavors and nuances like the finest wines in his cellars. He grows five to ten hot pepper varieties, perhaps a dozen heirloom tomatoes, and herbs such as lemon verbena on the restaurant's roof during summer. Micro-greens, cilantro, beet greens, pea sprouts, and other herbs grow year-round in his light garden.

But It's More Than Taste

Another reason heirlooms, farmers' markets, and home gardens are growing in popularity is the fallout from the factory-farm model of food production. *Is our food supply safe?* That's a question many are asking. Nearly half of the 48 million food poisoning cases annually are caused by vegetables and fruit, according to The Centers for Disease Control. When acres and acres of the same hybrid vegetable variety are planted, however, they can become hosts for salmonella, *which has genetically altered itself to attack that specific hybrid*. Chicken feed, which is mostly corn, is also susceptible. When fed to poultry, the bird becomes the incubator of the bacteria and passes it along in its eggs and meat when slaughtered. Planting a variety of heirlooms ensures that salmonella or any other pathogen will not adapt itself to infect all plants. The home gardener can also control other factors like fertilizer and water that may also be contaminated. And, if you save your seeds from year to year, you'll never have to worry about a clean, healthy seed supply.

Diversity for the Future

By planting heirlooms, *diversity* is maintained too. When you grow a plant from heirloom seed and save that seed, you are participating in a tradition that dates back more than 10,000 years. Our grandparents and *their* grandparents grew these varieties. Often the seeds were prized possessions carried to the New World when they emigrated. These links to our heritage are also reminders of what dinner tasted like at Grandma's or Aunt Opal's decades ago. Plant three or four kinds of potatoes, for instance, and experience the differences in flavors, aromas, and colors among them. That diversity isn't available in the produce section, where all potatoes seem to taste the same. In the last 40 years, one corporation has bio-engineered hybrid vegetable seeds that account for up to 40 percent of the crops planted globally. These few varieties can hold the world's food supply hostage, as evidenced by the 1970s when corn blight that killed 70 percent of the corn harvest. Diversity and taste are being driven to extinction in the names of profit and control. That's one of the reasons farmers' markets are increasing in number almost exponentially. Consumers want *more* than cookie-cutter, pale red, hard tomatoes and pre-packaged wilted lettuce mixes. Well, guess what? You *can* have more.

Save Money and Time

Listen to this: Heirloom gardening is less expensive than planting hybrids. That is important in any type of economy. Saved seeds cost nothing, seeds traded with others only require postage, and purchased heirloom seeds may cost less than hybrids. Did you know synthetic fertilizers are petroleum-based? Their manufacture contributes to global pollution, as well as maintains our dependence on oil. Hybrid seeds require large amounts of expensive fertilizers, adding to the cost of growing them and furthering our planet's dependence on oil. Heirlooms, on the other hand, require little fertilizer. Usually compost or composted cow manure is enough for them. Some vegetables and fruits don't need any added fertilizer because nitrogen encourages excess foliage production at the expense of vegetable or fruit formation.

If you plant correctly and take steps to prevent disease and insect problems, large, healthy crops are easy to grow—meaning less time has to be spent in the garden. Start with healthy soil that has plenty of organic matter such as compost, shredded leaves, and worms in it. The wigglers are signs that the soil is fertile and not laced with poisons. Space plants wide, at least twice the recommended distance, so that air flows freely around foliage. Diseases such as mildew don't like dry leaves and moving air. Mulch the garden bed thickly, right up to plant stems (but not touching them). At least 2 inches of straw or compost will suppress any fungal spores that may splash up from the soil to infect plants. Weed seeds are smothered too. The most important thing you can do, and it's the least expensive of all, is to walk through the garden every day to see if there is a problem. Take care of it immediately, before a small thing becomes an epidemic.

Why Save Seeds?

The genetics of seeds change continuously, even with heirlooms. Weather, length of day, lack of soil fertility, or something as bucolic as squirrels frolicking among melon vines make a plant adapt in order to survive. In the case of the squirrels, they can pierce the rind of a ripening muskmelon, causing it to rot. Melons with thicker and harder rinds will survive and their seeds will mature to become the next generation. Climate change, whether you believe in it or not, has much to do with seeds adapting and changing. That's why hot-summer crops such as corn have evolved into different varieties that thrive even in chilly Duluth, Minnesota, or Burlington, Vermont. Tomatoes are an excellent example of new colors and tastes appearing constantly among heirlooms. Tom Wagner, of Tater'Mater Seeds and creator of many Class III heirloom tomatoes, says he loves recessive genes. They pop up in saved seeds now and then, with a new color or shape. He's currently working to stabilize a blue tomato that appeared in a field full of black tomato plants. I've saved the seeds of Black Zebra tomatoes for many years. One summer, a plant produced green tear-drop-shaped fruit with yellow flesh instead of the usual chestnut-and-green-striped fruit that has red flesh! Saving heirloom seeds is always an adventure!. You can always count on saved seed to produce a healthy, abundant crop with minimum cost—no matter how bad the weather and insect or disease infestations.

The world of heirlooms is exciting—come with me as we explore it.

Doreen

Savoring the Rich Flavor of the Past

Flavor is everything.

Whether it's the citrusy, honey-spice in every crunchy bite of an Ashmead's Kernel apple or the nuanced acid-sweet tones of mahogany Black Krim tomatoes from Russia, heirlooms deliver far more flavor than any hybrid. Flavor is pronounced, layered, aromatic, and sublime in these vegetables, herbs, and fruits of our ancestors. That's important to healthy eaters, those with refined palates, and many just now discovering what food should *really* taste like.

Heirlooms also offer colors, shapes, textures, and perfumes not found in hybrids, which have lost those traits by growers who bred them out in exchange for uniformity of size and a long shelf life. Potatoes, for instance, burst with a nutty sweetness accompanied by the flinty notes of a well-crafted Chablis. Ordinary hybrid potatoes lack that flavor complexity because they have been bred to be the background for other flavors, such as gravy or cheese, or to be fried and heavily salted. Hollow, ruffled tomatoes like Schimmeig Stoo, creamy yellow Boothby's Blond cucumbers, and vivid burgundy Chinese Yard-Long snap beans won't be found in grocery store produce sections. Tree-ripened Chojuro Asian pears waft an aroma redolent with jasmine, cinnamon, and molasses. Their exquisite fruit tastes of butterscotch with a floral note of spice. You won't find them in grocery stores either.

But you *can* find these gifts of our heritage at fruit orchards and at a growing number of seasonal farmers' markets. But why stop there? You can grow your own. It's easy to add a miniature apple tree or two to a townhouse lot, grow 200-year-old speckled Forellenschus lettuce in a pot, or plant a 6-foot row of Pineapple tomatoes and Lemon cucumbers edged with Lettuce Leaf basil against a fence. Or plant heirlooms among the annuals, perennials, roses, and shrubs in your flower gardens; mixing ornamentals and heirlooms is increasingly popular as consumers realize the exquisite colors and flavors heirlooms offer. The heirlooms featured in this book are easy to find, plus there are plenty of tips for selecting, growing, and enjoying these jewels from our collective ancestry. Whatever you choose to do, I *promise* you will be glad you've tried heirlooms.

What Is an Heirloom?

In the fruit world, an heirloom is any plant variety in existence before 1900. Fruit trees, shrubs, and vines are propagated by cuttings from the original plant—not by seeds. But vegetables reproduce by seed, as do most herbs. The heirloom designation applies only to seeds in existence before 1940. They must be open-pollinated, meaning the seeds reproduce the same vegetable or herb as the parent 95 percent of the time (called "come true"). There are three sub-classifications.

I. Varieties in existence before 1940 used by canneries, growers, and seed producers. Most of these went out of favor because hybrids shipped better and were consistent in size, color, and harvest time. World War II, and the need to feed a war-decimated world afterwards, triggered rampant hybridization. Canneries required uniform size and sugar content. Expansion of the rail system and other distribution methods also gave rise to the ability to offer hybrid tomatoes in January for Chicago grocery stores and apples hybridized for a long shelf-life in Miami. Tom Thumb lettuce and Red Alpine strawberries are examples of Class I.

II. Varieties in existence before 1940 that were handed down from generation to generation by families, ethnic communities, or regional farmers. Examples of Class II are Chiogga beets and Brandywine tomatoes.

III. The open-pollinated offspring of two heirlooms that is stabilized through the F-6 or greater generation—that means seeds were saved at least six growing cycles in a row. The Purple Dragon carrot, created by Dr. John Navazio, and Tom Wagner's Green Zebra tomato are examples of Class III.

Ancient Roots

Heirlooms are not only luscious in taste and appearance, but many have histories richer than some countries. Lettuce, for instance, was first cultivated by the ancient Egyptians as part of their religious rituals and was quickly adopted by marauding Romans as an appetizer. Carrots and apples grew wild in the craggy mountains of Afghanistan. Carrots were purple colored to survive the strong ultraviolet light at the high elevations in the mountains. Early hunter-gatherers 7,000 years ago subsisted on the apples and any small game, such as voles, they could kill.

Originally, tomatoes were yellow and grew wild in Peru. The early Aztecs cultivated them, and tomatoes spread to Europe in the sixteenth century as Spanish conquistadores, returning from treasure hunting in Mexico, introduced them. Most Europeans believed, however, these new fruits were poisonous and wouldn't eat them. They dubbed tomatoes "poison apples" because aristocrats got sick or died after eating them. But the real reason was the wealthy used pewter plates, which contained high quantities of lead. The acid in tomatoes caused the lead to leach, which led to lead poisoning. The poor only had plates made of wood so they were able to eat tomatoes without getting sick. Tomatoes finally gained wide acceptance in the 1880s with the invention of pizza in Italy. (What a relief! Can you imagine a cuisine without the tomato?)

Taste Is the Reason

As fascinating as the history of edibles is, the deciding factor for me to grow heirlooms in the last two decades has been taste. Each heirloom, from an Alpine strawberry to Blue Lake pole bean, possesses a distilled intense essence layered with nuances you won't get with a hybrid. Hybrids dominate our food chain because of their uniform size, maturity date, and inherent disease resistance, which has been bred into them. But there is an underbelly to disease resistence. Gene splicing and the insertion of foreign genes from animals and petrochemicals are the current widespread trends toward "building" the perfect vegetable. Flavor has flown the coop, so to speak, in return for production strengths. Meanwhile, we food lovers come up empty on taste and even nutrition. That's why I wrote this book, to let you know that flavor hasn't disappeared. I hope you grow a few heirlooms to experience their unique, concentrated tastes, and I also hope you seek them out at organic grocery stores and farmers' markets. Regardless of how you obtain them, I know you'll quickly agree that heirlooms cannot be surpassed when it comes to flavor.

If you decide to grow heirlooms, please share your harvest with the hungry. Vegetables such as squash, cucumbers, and beans produce huge crops all at once, and you can quickly be overwhelmed. Rather than waste the excess, share. To find the nearest food pantry or soup kitchen, go to www.gardenwriters.org/par for listings in your area. I must disclose that I have a vested interest, as I've been involved with an organization called Plant a Row for the Hungry since its inception in the 1990s, and I've served on its board. We collect more than one million pounds of vegetables and fruit every year to help the hungry.

The Heirloom Revival Movement

The return to growing heirlooms didn't happen overnight. Gardeners started questioning the decline in diversity of available vegetables in the early 1970s. The bean and tomato varieties their parents planted were no longer available through seed catalogs, dropped in favor of hybrids whose seeds couldn't be saved for the following year's crop. Corporations producing these hybrids lobbied hard for a decade in Washington D.C. for the right to patent their hybrid vegetables and fruit. President Richard Nixon signed a bill into law in 1970 stating that a gardener would have to buy the seeds or cloned plants (in the case of fruit) from the producer, paying premium prices. And seeds that were saved wouldn't produce the same vegetable when planted the next year. At the same time, the economy was in shambles, prices were soaring, and many started planting vegetable gardens to tame their rising food bills. That extra expense of hybrid seeds and transplants, and the large amount of fertilizer that hybrids require, added to the economic squeeze most families felt.

The Founding Fathers (and Mothers)

Alan Kapuler, Ph.D. of Corvallis, Oregon, felt the economic pinch as he planted his first garden to help feed his family. Educated in plant genetics, he knew plenty of open-pollinated vegetable seeds existed, but getting his hands on them wasn't easy. It was then he started his journey to find, save, and perpetuate the crops of the past. A retail seed company that would make heirlooms available to more people than any other method was needed, he felt. He started Peace Seeds in 1975, and it's now a public-domain plant-breeding venture that develops open-pollinated varieties from heirloom genes. Peace Seeds became the business model for Seeds of Change, one of the largest retail sources of heirloom seeds and plants today. Kapuler was one of the founders of the organization in 1989.

Seeds of Change brought together academics and gardeners who researched, grew, and preserved ancient varieties of vegetables, herbs, and fruit, especially those in the Southwestern states and bordering territories of Mexico. Kenny Ausubel, Gabriel Howearth, Richard Pecoraro, Julie Spelletich, and Emigdio Ballon, a Quechua Bolivian Indian agronomist, were among the founders. They began planting open-pollinated seeds they had collected on a small farm in Gila, New Mexico, in 1989. In 1996, the Seeds of Change farm moved closer to its Santa Fe office, to a 6-acre plot of floodplain along the Rio Grande River in El Guique, New Mexico. Originally land that was cultivated by the ancient Tewa Indians, the farm has been developed into productive fields with intensive cover cropping, compost applications, and minimal tilling. This is where Seeds of Change conducts research and produces some of the seeds they sell in their catalog. They also have a state-of-the-art seed cleaning facility.

About the same time Alan Kapuler planted his first vegetable garden, a young couple in Iowa, Diane Ott Whealy and Kent Whealy, pondered the future of vegetable and flower varieties handed down through generations, like the ones Diane had recently received from her terminally ill grandfather. Baptist Ott gave Diane seeds of two garden plants: Grandpa Ott's morning glory and German Pink tomato, which his parents had brought from Bavaria when they immigrated to St. Lucas, Iowa, in the 1870s. Diane and Kent had been noticing a rapid decline in the diversity of seeds available for gardens. They knew if Grandpa Ott's seeds were to be available for future generations, they had to plant them, save the seeds, and share them with other

gardeners. It was on that note that Kent, especially, because he had the tools as a journalist, researched what it would take to collect, propagate, and save thousands of heirlooms for future generations. The couple started Seed Savers Exchange (SSE) in 1975 as a nonprofit grassroots network of gardeners, fruit growers, plant collectors, and chefs.

Today, SSE, based at its 890-acre Heritage Farm in Decorah, Iowa, permanently maintains more than 25,000 endangered vegetable varieties. Seed Savers is the largest non-government seed bank in the United States. Most of the seeds have been brought to North America by SSE members' ancestors, who emigrated from Europe, the Middle East, Asia, and other parts of the world. In many of these places, seed saving is the norm, rather than buying packets of hybrid seeds. Heirloom seeds from Native American, Mennonite, Amish, Dunkard, Hutterite, and Cajun gardeners are also included in the collection.

SSE members exchange seeds with one another; a sizable catalog for members only is published every winter. Membership fees are nominal, and members are encouraged to share the seeds they grow. The organization maintains a retail website and mails a catalog to non-members to permit them to purchase seeds. This selection is a small percentage of what is available to members, but this catalog is an excellent place to start.

Heirloom Specialists

In the mid-1960s, a group of like-minded fruit growers started corresponding with one another in a round-robin fashion. One person received a letter, added their comments and newest experiences about fruit varieties and growing them, and then mailed the letter on to the next person on the list. This humble exchange became the North American Fruit Explorers (NAFEX) in 1967. Founding members Milo Gibson and Fred Janson took some of the most interesting information from these round-robin exchanges and assembled it into a small quarterly digest. The first issue of *POMONA* was published in late summer of 1967. The organization has grown to 3,000 members in the United States and Canada and many foreign countries. Evaluating antique fruits versus hybrids for ease of growth, taste, and appeal is one of the top activities of the organization. Gardeners from Vancouver and Boston may grow the same antique apple, such as Cox's Orange Pippen, but it will perform differently in the diverse climates and its flavor will vary too. NAFEX has a website where you can sign up for their listserv, which has become the Internet version of the old round-robin letters. Anyone can participate in these exchanges or merely lurk, learning much about a fruit they may anticipate planting. Go to www.nafex.org for more information.

Mahina Dees and Gary Nabhan were working for the "Meals for Millions" program on the Tohono O'odham Nation south of Tucson, Arizona, in the early 1980s, where they helped establish community gardens to feed the hungry. Some of the elders they worked with commented that, while the broccoli and radish seeds were fine, what they *really* wanted were vegetables that had been grown by the generations before them. No one had seeds for these heirloom varieties. That request sparked the realization that with the advent of industrial agriculture, most of the once-prominent crops of the area had been lost. The pair, along with their spouses, Barney T. Burns and Karen Reichhardt, founded Native Seed SEARCH in January 1983 to find, document, propagate, and distribute the adapted and diverse agricultural crops (and their wild relatives) that once grew in the American Southwest and northwestern Mexico. The regional and cultural focus of their seed collection is what makes the nonprofit organization unique from many other seed banks. "If we went out today to gather the seeds in our collection, we couldn't do it," said Barney Burns. "They're not there."

Native Seed SEARCH operates a 60-acre farm in Patagonia, Arizona, where it maintains 1,800 heirloom varieties. Half of these are the "three sisters"—corn, bean, and squash. An additional 48 species of wild and crop plants are also maintained, including rarities such as red-seeded amaranth (used to dye piki bread), black-seeded sunflowers (used as a dye), drought-tolerant beans grown in the hottest region of northwestern Mexico, Sonoran panic grass (once thought extinct), lemon basil, and red-seeded watermelon. This organization has a large membership that contributes seeds and/or information, plus it distributes retail seed catalogs via print and the Internet. Members receive a 10 percent discount on their order, and Native Americans can become members for free. There is also a store in Tucson that showcases native seeds and other products.

An Heirloom Manifesto

Nothing tastes better than a hot, buttered ear of corn eaten outdoors on a perfect summer afternoon. But that bucolic picture isn't accurate. This heirloom of the Americas now feeds mostly livestock; or it is processed into dynamite, duct tape, and food additives; or it bolsters our international trade balance. In the last 100 years, corn has become the dominant crop grown commercially in this country. With government subsidies to encourage farmers, millions of pounds are grown, but less than 2 percent is sold in the produce section or made into processed food such as corn chips.

Industrial uses for corn include filler for plastics, packing materials, insulating materials, adhesives, chemicals, explosives, paint, paste, abrasives, dyes, insecticides, pharmaceuticals, organic acids, solvents, rayon, antifreeze, and soaps. By 2000, corn fed to livestock was 60 percent of the annual harvest, 22 percent was exported, 6 percent was used for high-fructose corn sweetener, and 6 percent was processed for ethanol.

Compare the current statistics to 1930, when virtually the world's entire corn crop consisted of open-pollinated heirloom varieties whose seeds could be saved and replanted. By 1965, about 95 percent of all U.S. corn planted consisted of hybrid varieties. In that 35-year period, scientists created hybrids that yielded more and required less water. Machines replaced muscles, so farmers wanted corn with uniform ripening times and stalk height to accommodate mechanized harvesting. To boost yields per acre even further, hybrids were bred to consume as much fertilizer as possible. Over this period, *fertilizer use increased 1,700 percent*. Recently, the emphasis has been on breeding genetically altered corn with disease and insect resistance. There is even a corn variety with built-in sterility—a "terminator" gene—inserted into it that prevents any saved seed from germinating (a United Nations treaty in 2000 prevented these seeds from reaching the market). Breeding became so specific by 1970 that only six hybrid varieties were planted commercially. Within a year, a new strain of leaf blight appeared, and these mono-cropped corn plants died across the nation. There is still little diversity among commercial corn varieties.

What can you do? Maintain diversity in your garden by planting corn whose seed can be saved and replanted. Open-pollinated varieties mutate to defend themselves against disease attacks, unlike hybrids. Or buy locally grown, non-hybrid varieties at farmers' markets to keep heirlooms in production. There *is* a choice, and it's up to you to make it.

Vegetables

Chapter One

Beans

Beans are diverse, ranging from juicy, sweet green beans to dried soup beans to a shiny, purple-podded one that kills! Green beans are called string beans because years ago on the old varieties a fibrous string ran along the seam of the bean. The string was noticeable when you snapped off the ends. That snapping noise is the reason for its other nickname of "snap bean." But not all string or snap beans are green; yellow ones are called wax beans due to their waxy skin and lack of chlorophyll. Others are red, purple, or combinations of colors, such as Dragon's Tongue, a yellow heirloom streaked with purple. All types grow as a short, fast-maturing bush or a vine that is trained upward on a pole or trellis. Pole beans mature later than bush plants but both types produce dry or shelling beans. You should harvest string beans young for the best, most tender flavor. Seeds left inside the remaining pods dry and are ready for shelling about four to six weeks later. That's what makes any bean plant a valuable addition to heirloom gardens: you'll get two different crops from one plant; one for fresh eating and the other to store for winter meals.

But it's green snap or string beans that most people think of as beans. They've been a favorite of Americans for the garden and plate since the 1830s. Dried beans, which are the mature seeds in the pod, have been around since 8,000 B.C., feeding the world's population. Dried beans contain 22 percent protein and are packed with minerals and vitamin A. However, beans are missing certain amino acids, which prevents them from being a complete protein source. Cooked beans eaten with corn, which contains the missing nutrients plus a whopping 44 percent of additional protein, are a "complete" protein. This duo has been served for centuries and continues to be served where inexpensive protein sources are important. Freshly made corn tortillas spread with mashed pinto beans that have been seasoned with garlic, cilantro, and chiles is a tasty example. *Mmmm.*

In the Kitchen with Doreen

Beans

Dilled beans are simple to make and a good way to use extras. Pick and wash enough beans to fill one-half of a quart jar. Add two peeled garlic cloves, two heads of fresh dill weed, and 1 teaspoon sea salt. Fill the jar with 1 cup white vinegar and top it off with distilled water. Refrigerate. Start enjoying the crisp pickled beans five days later.

Freshly harvested beans have the best flavor, but they can be stored in the refrigerator for up to five days. Don't wash them until you are ready to cook the beans.

Dishes made with dried beans taste better the day after you cook them. The beans and their juices thicken and flavors deepen. My favorite dried bean dish is an Easter ham bone cooked for hours with Jacob's Cattle beans, onions, garlic, and rosemary. Delicious!

Use your crockpot to cook dried beans while you work. Soak them overnight and then cook 8 to 10 hours on the low setting. For every 1 cup of dried beans, add 3 cups of water.

Green Beans with Tomatoes and Olives

Makes 4 servings

1 pound green beans, trimmed
½ cup halved grape tomatoes
½ cup pitted and halved kalamata olives
2 teaspoons extra-virgin olive oil
Kosher salt
Freshly ground pepper
Lemon wedges

In a large pot of boiling salted water, cook the green beans until crisp-tender, about 3 minutes. Drain and rinse under cold water. Halve the beans and place in a large bowl. Add the tomatoes, olives, and oil and toss gently. Season with salt and pepper. Serve with the lemon wedges.

Mediterranean Salad

Makes 8 servings

2 pounds small red potatoes, unpeeled
1½ pounds fresh green beans
1 recipe Herb Dressing, divided
    (recipe follows)
2 heads romaine lettuce
6 (3-ounce) packages albacore tuna, flaked
2 ounces Italian hard salami,
    sliced into strips
5 hard-cooked eggs, quartered
5 plum tomatoes, cut into wedges, or
    1 (8-ounce) container grape tomatoes
1 cup sliced black olives

Cook the potatoes in boiling water to cover for 15 minutes until tender, then drain. Cool slightly and cut into slices.

Cook the green beans in boiling water to cover for 3 minutes and drain. Plunge into ice water to stop the cooking process.

Toss together the potato slices, green beans, and ½ cup of the dressing in a large bowl. Chill for at least 30 minutes.

Tear 1 head of the lettuce into bite-size pieces. Line a platter with the leaves of the remaining head of lettuce. Arrange the potato mixture over the lettuce. Top with the torn lettuce pieces.

Mound the tuna in the center of the greens. Arrange the salami around the tuna. Place the eggs and tomato wedges on the salad. Sprinkle with the olives. Serve with the remaining dressing.

Herb Dressing

Makes 1½ cups

1 cup olive oil
½ cup red wine vinegar
2 green onions, chopped
2 teaspoons dried basil
2 teaspoons dried marjoram
2 teaspoons dried oregano
2 teaspoons dried thyme
½ teaspoon salt
½ teaspoon freshly ground pepper

Whisk together all the ingredients in a small bowl.

Bush

Pencil Pod Black Wax

Pick these long-producing wax beans young for the best sweet, big-bean flavor. Although best eaten fresh, this heirloom also freezes and cans well, retaining much of its essence. This bean has been standard in American gardens for over 100 years and does well in areas of hot summers and climates.

(52 Days)

Black Valentine

Slender, green beans are harvested at six weeks and have a distinctive, full-bean flavor. Black dried beans for soups are ready to harvest about a month later. The seeds germinate well, even in cool soil. It was planted in American gardens before 1850.

(42 to 70 Days)

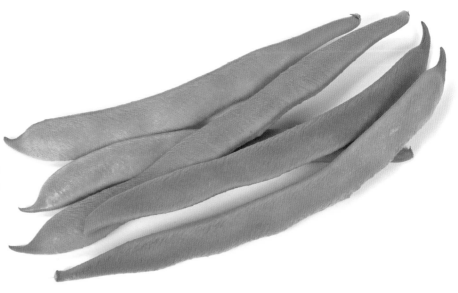

Bountiful Stringless

The pods are bright green, straight, and flat; bite into one when you are picking for a crisp, juicy sweet treat. Developed in Genesee, New York, in 1898, Bountiful Stringless is also called Bountiful in some catalogs.

(41 to 52 Days)

Romano

Romano beans, 6-inch-long flat beans that originated in Italy, have a meaty, juicy taste that sets them apart from other snap beans. The compact bush plants produce until frost and hold their pods well off the ground. Grown commercially before 1940, this bush version is an open-pollinated offspring of Romano pole beans.

(55 to 60 Days)

Triomphe de Farcy

Its green pods are long, thin filet types that have a distinctive, rich flavor. Pick when they're less than 6 inches long and harvest at least every other day for the finest flavor and texture. The bright color holds nicely if the pods are briefly steamed. This French heirloom dates to 1892 and tolerates hot and dry conditions. Also called Triumph de Farcy.

(48 to 55 Days)

Dragon's Tongue

Packed with a big-bean flavor, these gorgeous pods are a creamy yellow artistically streaked with vivid purple. Beans are long and flat with pointed ends. You must steam the beans to retain their color; if boiled, their streaks disappear or turn a fuzzy gray. Dragon's Tongue comes from the Netherlands.

(57 to 65 Days)

Pole

Rattlesnake

Harvest Rattlesnake early for a very sweet snap bean but leave the remaining pods to mature into buff-and-dark-brown-speckled soup beans. Its robust vines produce cascades of 8-inch, rounded light green pods streaked with purple like the skin of a rattlesnake, hence its name. A Native American heirloom, originated by the Cherokee, Rattlesnake beans are also known as Preacher Beans.

(75 Days)

Blue Lake

Early, prolific, and extra sweet, Blue Lake's tender pods are long, rounded, and slender. Plants produce throughout the summer if the pods are kept picked. Blue Lake vines easily reach 6 feet and produce pods in clusters of five or six, making picking easy. Blue Lake has been the variety of choice for canning by home gardeners and commercial growers for nearly 100 years.

(60 to 65 Days)

Kentucky Wonder

The tastiest pole-type string bean according to many, Kentucky Wonder pods are extra long, about 10 inches, and grow in clusters. They're sweet, have no fiber, and are ready to pick about 2 months after seeds sprout. The white or tan dried beans can be harvested a month or two later. Called Old Homestead when it was introduced in 1864, Kentucky Wonder has proven to be a garden standard for more than a century due to its taste and productivity.

(65 to 90 Days)

Chinese Red Noodle

Chinese Red Noodle is very long—up to 22 inches—thin, and an unusual garnet red color. The beans are sweet and tender. Beans lose their red color when cooked, but will retain it if they're stir-fried or sautéed. They're good deep-fried and sprinkled with toasted black sesame seeds. Grown in America since the 1800s, Red Noodle's origin is mainland China, and it came to the United States with Chinese immigrants who were brought here to build railroad systems in western states.

(80 Days)

Purple Hyacinth

Grown by many as a vigorous ornamental vine, this ancient bean takes three months or more to produce neon purple, flat, curved beans. Pick Purple Hyacinth pods when they are very young and sweet. Use them in stir-fry dishes and steamed with other colorful vegetables, such as yellow crookneck squash and carrots, for a stunning medley. Older pods quickly turn fibrous. Do *not* eat the dried beans; they contain hydrogen cyanide. The gorgeous purple flowers that precede the beans attract butterflies and hummingbirds. Also called Indian Bean and Egyptian Bean, this heirloom is a food crop throughout the tropics, especially in Africa. Thomas Jefferson grew them, and the beans were found in seed catalogs as early as 1802.

(100+ Days)

Dry Shelling

Black Coco

Their flavor is rich and nutty with a hint of epazote. Pick Black Coco for string beans at 60 days maturity; more pods will appear as this bush plant is vigorous and productive. The resulting chocolate-black dried beans cook quickly and make excellent refried beans.

(85 Days)

Tiger's Eye

Tiger's Eye has beautiful dry beans: orange with dark maroon swirling stripes that resemble a tiger's eye. It tastes similar to a pinto bean, but is creamier in texture. Easy to grow and harvest, Tiger's Eye originated either in Chile or Argentina. It's a bush type, with a tendency to vine; plants grow about 2 feet tall and sometimes as wide. The beans can also be picked at an earlier stage and eaten as a snap bean.

(85 to 95 Days)

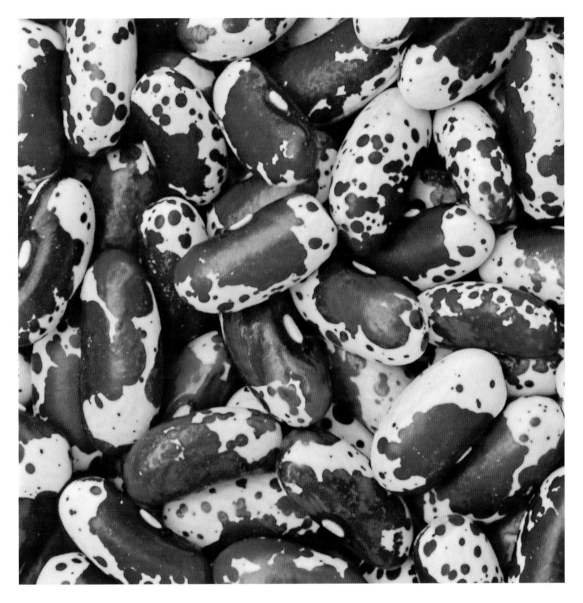

Jacob's Cattle

This attractive, New England favorite for baked beans has a nutty, creamy taste even after hours of cooking. Bush-type plants bear numerous pods that each hold five white seeds speckled with maroon-brown. Jacob's Cattle is also called Trout and Dalmatian.

(80 to 100 Days)

Chapter Two

Beets and Swiss Chard

"Bloody turnip" isn't an appetizing name to bestow upon a vegetable, but that's what the Greeks and Romans called beets. Botanically, they referred to the bulb as *beta*. The names "beetroot" and "beet" evolved as red pigments began to dominate. Up until 300 A.D., when the red and white beetroots appeared in Italian gardens, most beets were black; only a few were white.

A German chemist in 1747 found that white beetroots contain sucrose, the same sweet compound found in sugar cane. Even though it takes 100 pounds of sugar beets to produce 5 pounds of sugar; by 1880, 50 percent of the world's sugar came from beets, despite its low conversion yield. That percentage was achieved in some part because, during the Napoleonic Wars, the British blockade of the supply lines prevented cane sugar from reaching France. Napoleon decreed that France would grow thousands of hectares (roughly one-half an acre) for the production of sugar beets. Once the blockade ended, sugar cane once again was imported into France and the rest of the Continent. Today about 30 percent of the sugar consumed worldwide is still made from sugar beets.

Beets and Swiss chard are the same vegetable, each a variation created over time by natural selection from numerous genetic crosses and mutations in response to climate and growing conditions. As early as 2,000 B.C., the Greeks and Romans grew two colors of green and a ruby red chard. Leaf beets, or Swiss chard as we call it, don't have the same colorful roots as the beetroot or sugar beet, which forms a bulb instead of fleshy stalks like Swiss chard. Swiss chard got its name from a Swiss botanist named Koch who, in the nineteenth century, named the vegetable in honor of his homeland, even though it originated in the Mediterranean region.

Use Swiss chard as you would spinach, but it's more tender and doesn't have the mouth-drying iron taste that spinach has. It's a nutritional powerhouse, full of vitamins A, C, and K, as well as magnesium, iron, potassium, and fiber. Give it a try—you'll be glad you did!

In the Kitchen with Doreen

Beets and Swiss Chard

Harvest beets when the roots are about 2 inches in diameter and tender. As they grow larger, the flesh becomes tough and a fibrous yellow core forms.

Beet greens are edible and are filled with vitamins and antioxidants. Chop up some greens and simmer them in chicken soup for a flavor and nutrient boost.

Harvest Swiss chard by cutting or snapping off the outer leaves. The plant is a rosette, meaning it grows new leaves from the center.

Sauté chopped Swiss chard in olive oil with a couple of mashed garlic cloves for a colorful, nutritious side dish.

Instead of celery, dice Swiss chard ribs for tuna or chicken salad. Their crunchy flavor is similar, and they are not stringy like celery!

Sauté chopped Swiss chard with slices of Italian sausage and season with smoky paprika and lemon zest for a delicious and quick low-carbohydrate dish packed with antioxidants.

Harvest a leaf or two from each beet every week for fresh salad greens. Bulls Blood and Chiogga leaves have vivid red variegations, which make them attractive and nutritious additions to salads.

Wash harvested beets *gently*, as their skin is thin. Steam, boil, or roast them with their skins on to retain all the nutrients; the skins can be gently rubbed off when the cooked beets are cool.

Throw some beet halves on the grill along with purple cauliflower slices (brushed with olive oil) when you prepare your next steak. This combination is one of my family's favorite ways to eat their five daily servings of vegetables!

Roasted Beets

Makes 6 servings

12 beets
3 tablespoons extra-virgin
    olive oil
1½ teaspoons minced fresh
    thyme leaves
2 teaspoons kosher salt, plus
    additional for sprinkling
1 teaspoon freshly ground
    pepper, plus additional for
    sprinkling
2 tablespoons raspberry vinegar
Juice of 1 large orange

Preheat the oven to 400 degrees F.

Remove the tops and the roots of the beets and peel each one with a vegetable peeler. Cut the beets into 1½-inch chunks. (Small beets can be halved, medium ones cut in quarters, and large ones cut in eighths.)

Place the cut beets on a baking sheet and toss with the oil, thyme, salt, and pepper. Roast for 35 to 40 minutes, turning once or twice with a spatula, until the beets are tender. Remove from the oven, transfer to a large bowl, and immediately toss with the vinegar and orange juice. Sprinkle with salt and pepper and serve warm.

Swiss Chard Quiche Frittata

Makes 8 servings

1 teaspoon olive oil
2 cups coarsely chopped
    Swiss chard
Salt
Freshly ground pepper
4 eggs
1 cup milk
¼ cup minced fresh chives
2½ cups shredded sharp
    Cheddar cheese

Preheat the oven to 375 degrees F. Spray a pie pan with nonstick cooking spray.

Heat the oil in a large skillet, add the Swiss chard, and sauté until the stems are barely tender. Season with salt and pepper.

Beat the eggs in a large bowl. Stir in the milk, chives, and cheese. Add the chard and combine. Pour into the prepared pan.

Bake for 35 to 45 minutes, until the frittata is golden brown and no liquid seeps out when it is cut with a knife tip.

Beet

Chiogga

Also called the "candy cane" beet, this Italian heirloom, introduced to the U.S. in 1840, has red-and-white concentric rings that are decorative and sweet-flavored in salads and on relish trays. When cooked, the circles lose their definition and the beets turn an overall pink. The green tops also have pink striping. Chiogga is easy to grow and not fussy about soil.

(52 Days)

Bull's Blood

An heirloom from the Netherlands known for its intense flavor and breathtaking color, Bull's Blood's foliage is a stunning dark red-purple. Scarlet beets are sweet, a robust red, and taste best when they're harvested young. They retain their tender sweetness when pickled, canned, or steamed. The deep red leaves are sweeter than radicchio and tasty in salads. Many commercial mesclun mixes use this heirloom variety's leaves. Introduced to the U.S. in 1840, many gardeners grew Bull's Blood, and still do, for its stunning foliage; the glossy leaves reach 18 inches high. It's an exceptional dual-purpose heirloom.

(35 to 60 Days)

Golden Beet

One of the sweetest beets available, the orange bulbs are very fine textured and turn golden yellow when cooked. They are best eaten fresh, but Golden Beet stores well and is also good pickled. This heirloom dates to 1828, when it was popular all over Europe (and still is). Golden Beet's seed germination rate is lower than other beet varieties, so sow seeds thickly (three times as much as you normally would).

(55 to 60 Days)

Detroit Dark Red

Introduced to the U.S. in 1892, Detroit Dark Red has a sweet, intense flavor and fine-grained flesh. It's excellent cooked, pickled, or canned. The plants are naturally mildew resistant. Harvest when the roots are 3 inches in diameter. These perfectly round beets have been the favorite variety of gardeners and commercial growers for over 100 years. Detroit Dark Red does well grown in a container.

(60 Days)

Swiss Chard

Five Color Silver Beet

Neon shades of red, pink, orange, yellow, and silver color the ribs of this Swiss chard, making it a beautiful addition to any garden or plate. Ribs turn green when they're boiled; steam leaves lightly to retain their colors. Enjoy this vegetable raw in salads, as you would spinach. The plants are easy to grow, and you can harvest new leaves over a long period. Mature plants tolerate heat and cold without losing their flavor. Silver Beet is the Australian name for Swiss chard. Five Color is also known as Rainbow chard in Europe, where it originated two centuries ago.

(55 to 60 Days)

Swiss Chard

Rhubarb Chard

The highly colored stalks of Rhubarb Chard closely resemble rhubarb, hence its alternate name of Ruby Red. This ancient ruby red variety has the mildest flavor of all chards. Admired by Aristotle, Rhubarb Chard was introduced into the U.S. in 1857. The current strain available is a Class III heirloom that was developed by Dr. John Navazio, who selected offspring with the best traits. This selective breeding has resulted in larger ribs and mildew-resistant plants.

(45 to 60 Days)

Chapter Three

Cabbage, Broccoli, Cauliflower, Kohlrabi, and Brussels Sprouts

The average person thinks of cabbage, broccoli, and other members of the Brassica family as different vegetables—they aren't. All are cabbages, from thumb-sized Brussels sprouts to purple cauliflower. Every form of cabbage will cross readily with another to produce new variations. For instance, cauliflower and broccoli are almost botanically identical, except that cauliflower doesn't form shoots or side heads after the main head has been harvested like broccoli does. Writer and philosopher Mark Twain opined, "Cauliflower is nothing but cabbage with a college education." Modern-day botanists think Brussels sprouts were created in the middle to late 1700s because of such a random cross of genes. The small-headed Milan cabbage, grown extensively in the Low Countries of Belgium where Brussels is located, was probably the parent. The name "Brussels sprouts" stuck.

The mother of all cabbage forms has been around forever, at least 6,000 years, and probably was first cultivated by the Celts in the form of the familiar leafy green head. Its genetic origins are in northwestern Europe, from coastal France to Holland and the southern English coastline. The Greeks and Romans grew cabbage, bestowing great status upon the vegetable. It was served with mint, coriander, raisins, wine, and green olives. Cabbage is considered Russia's national food; they eat about seven times as much cabbage as the average American. Because cabbage requires only three months' growing time, one acre of cabbage yields more edible vegetables than any other.

In more modern times, the W. Atlee Burpee Seed Company was founded on seeds from one cabbage, Surehead, in 1887. It was the size of a water bucket and averaged 30 pounds. A year later, Burpee offered thirty-one cabbage varieties in addition to Surehead, plus broccoli, cauliflower, Brussels sprouts, and kohlrabi. Most Americans aren't familiar with kohlrabi and have never tasted it. That cabbage variation, similar to a turnip, made its appearance in the U.S. around 1800, but it was first grown in Europe in the sixteenth century, where nobles and peasants alike savored it. Kohlrabi is not available in most grocery stores, so you have to grow it to enjoy its sweet, tender, nutty taste.

In the Kitchen with Doreen

Cabbage, Broccoli, Cauliflower, Kohlrabi, and Brussels Sprouts

Shredded raw cabbage makes a low-calorie alternative to rice or noodles in Oriental dishes. Try Szechwan beef or orange chicken over cabbage. The shreds catch the sauce and absorb flavors just like noodles and rice.

When cooking soups, stews, and casseroles, add broccoli at the end to retain its nutrients and preserve its flavor. If you don't, broccoli turns mushy and loses its flavor.

For a unique, scrumptious slaw, shred equal amounts of peeled kohlrabi and firm apples. Toss with minced mint leaves and balsamic vinegar. The salad is a fast way to dazzle dinner guests with texture, flavor, and curiosity about the ingredients.

Add a slice or two of white bread to the cooking water when boiling Brussels sprouts to eliminate its strong odor.

Peel kohlrabi before cooking; they have a much more delicate flavor than turnips.

Pick Brussels sprouts when they are young. The smaller the sprout, the more delicate the taste. Steam them until they're tender and top with garlic butter to enjoy this nutty, sweet vegetable at its best.

If you can't eat them after picking, refrigerate Brussels sprouts. If you don't, their leaves will turn yellow.

Broccoli has more nutrition in it than any other vegetable. The florets have more beta-carotene, vitamins, and minerals in them than the stems have. Steam or stir-fry the vegetable to retain its nutrients and for the best taste.

Keep cauliflower white when cooking it by adding a lemon slice to the pan. And, don't use aluminum or iron pots to cook the vegetable because cauliflower reacts with both metals, turning heads brown, yellow, or blue-green.

Cauliflower Gratin

Makes 4 to 6 servings

1 (3-pound) head of cauliflower,
   cut into large florets
4 tablespoons (½ stick) unsalted
   butter, divided
3 tablespoons all-purpose flour
2 cups hot milk
1 teaspoon kosher salt, plus
   additional for sprinkling
½ teaspoon freshly ground
   pepper, plus additional for
   sprinkling
¼ teaspoon grated nutmeg
¾ cup grated Gruyère
   cheese, divided
½ cup freshly grated
   Parmesan cheese
¼ cup fresh bread crumbs

Preheat the oven to 375 degrees F.

Cook the cauliflower florets in a large pot of boiling salted water for 5 to 6 minutes, until tender but still firm. Drain.

Meanwhile, melt 2 tablespoons of the butter in a medium saucepan over low heat. Add the flour and cook, stirring constantly with a wooden spoon, for 2 minutes. Pour the hot milk into the mixture and stir until it comes to a boil. Boil, whisking constantly, for 1 minute, until thickened. Remove from the heat and add the salt, pepper, nutmeg, ½ cup of the Gruyère cheese, and the Parmesan cheese.

Pour one-third of the sauce on the bottom of an 11 x 7-inch baking dish. Place the drained cauliflower on top of the sauce. In a small bowl, mix the crumbs with the remaining ¼ cup Gruyère cheese and sprinkle on top of the cauliflower. Melt the remaining 2 tablespoons butter and drizzle it onto the gratin. Sprinkle with salt and pepper. Bake for 25 to 30 minutes, until the top is browned. Serve hot or at room temperature.

Brussels Sprouts with Brown Butter

Makes 6 to 8 servings

2 pounds Brussels sprouts
2 quarts water
2 teaspoons salt
¼ cup butter
Minced garlic, to taste
Juice and zest of 1 lemon
Salt
White pepper

Trim the ends of the Brussels sprouts and cut in half, lengthwise. Combine the water and salt in a saucepan and bring to a boil. Add the Brussels sprouts and cook until tender but not mushy, about 7 minutes. Drain the Brussels sprouts. Heat the butter in a heavy skillet and add the sprouts and garlic, tossing to coat. Carefully allow the butter to brown, but do not let it burn. Add the lemon juice and zest, salt, and pepper. Serve immediately.

Cabbage

Drumhead Savoy

Crisp, tender, and extra sweet in flavor, Drumhead Savoy cabbage lacks the sulfurlike odor that others have when cooking. Heads are large (up to 6 pounds); coarsely crinkled leaves form compact heads on long stems. This heirloom came from France, where it was first listed in seed catalogs in 1891. It is the traditional cabbage Italians use to make minestrone soup. It's also called Perfection Drumhead Savoy.

(90 Days)

Red Drumhead

Very sweet like many red cabbages, Red Drumhead shines when served raw in salads and slaws. It retains its color when it's cooked. Harvest heads when they are about 7 inches in diameter for the best flavor. This heirloom came from Germany in the early 1860s, where it's called Roter Trummel.

(60 to 70 Days)

Cabbage

Early Jersey Wakefield

Mild and sweet, the heads form as a heart or cone shape with a well-rounded point. They weigh 2 to 4 pounds. Its leaves are sometimes tinged with pink. It was developed around 1850 as a field cabbage for farmers and dominated the market. Its early maturity made the heirloom the first crop to market in spring. Plant seeds early, as Early Jersey Wakefield doesn't like hot weather (the flavor turns unpleasantly strong flavored). It's also called True American.

(60 to 65 Days)

Kohlrabi

Early Purple Vienna

Early Purple Vienna's purple skin covers greenish white flesh, which tastes like a combination of a cauliflower and a turnip. Harvest this pretty globe that grows on top of the soil when it's young for its sweet and mild flavor. Early Purple Vienna and its sister Early White Vienna are the parents of all modern-day kohlrabi. First listed in American seed catalogs in 1863, this heirloom is still widely planted. Globes are slightly larger than Early White Vienna, and they mature a bit later.

(55 to 68 Days)

Early White Vienna

A mild, sweet, turniplike taste sets apart this kohlrabi. Its skin is light green and its flesh is greenish white. Superb raw or steamed, use bulbs when they are the size of an apple, before they become woody. Plant seeds directly in the ground 2 months before the first freeze is expected. Store bulbs in a cool, frost-free place for winter use. Early White Vienna was listed in seed catalogs by 1869, six years after Early Purple Vienna.

(45 to 55 Days)

Kohlrabi

Gigante

This 10-pound or heavier Czechoslovakian heirloom is very sweet, despite its size. Some grow to more than 50 pounds and the world record is 62 pounds, leaves included, according to Guinness World Records. Gigante's crisp white flesh remains tender with no tough, woody fibers. This kohlrabi is also called Gigante Winter, due to its long growing season, and Superschmeltz.

(130 Days)

Cauliflower

Early Snowball

Meaty, slightly sweet, and a farm standard since 1888, this heirloom boasts brilliant white heads on compact plants. It grows best in mild climates and as a fall-maturing plant in other climates. Smooth, 6- to 7-inch heads of tightly formed white curds are solid, crisp, and are of tender, excellent quality. Early Snowball was introduced to American gardeners in 1888 by Peter Henderson & Company.

(60 Days)

Purple Cape

Purple Cape has intense, exquisite taste and color. This heirloom was developed in South Africa in the 1700s and was introduced into England in 1808. It is hardier than other cauliflowers. Color is determined by the soil; the more acidic or lower the pH, the deeper purple the curds are. (The color fades to a grayish white when it's cooked.) To showcase its color, use the curds as crudités. The purple color is due to the antioxidant group anthocyanin, which can also be found in red cabbage and red wine.

(100 to 120 Days)

Brussels Sprouts

Rubine Red

Rubine Red's nutty, sweet, walnut-sized sprouts are frosted with crimson. These dwarf plants have uniformly deep purple-red leaves and stalks. It has been listed in seed catalogs since the late 1930s and is probably an open-pollinated selection of older red sprouts. This heirloom is a striking edible addition to ornamental gardens and a gourmet treat on dinner plates. Plants grow to 24 inches and perform best when they're planted early.

(85 to 120 Days)

Long Island Improved

The small sprouts on semidwarf plants (20 to 24 inches) are very sweet. Long Island Improved is very productive and can be left in the garden into winter as it tolerates temperatures to 25 degrees F. Frost actually improves its flavor. Long Island Improved has been grown since 1890 and is sometimes mistaken for Catskill, a strain developed by Arthur White of Arkport, New York, in 1941. The two are similar.

(85 to 115 Days)

Broccoli

Calabrese

This heirloom, which came to the U.S. with Italian immigrants in the 1820s, is full of old-time broccoli flavor—mustard nuances and robust taste. Large plants produce 3- to 6-inch, blue-green central heads, followed by numerous side shoots until frost.

(60 to 90 Days)

De Cicco

Another Italian heirloom brought to the U.S. in 1890 by immigrants, De Cicco produces prodigious numbers of tender, sweet side shoots. The main head is ready about 7 weeks after setting out transplants. Each compact plant produces a 3- to 6-inch blue-and-green speckled head with darker green side shoots. This heirloom, celebrated for its cut-and-come-again nature, starts producing early and continues producing shoots until frost for a long harvest.

(48 to 85 Days)

Romanesco

Pointed, whirled lime green heads have a firm, crunchy texture and abundant flavor; the florets are excellent when served raw in salads and as a crudités. Grown in northern Italy since the sixteenth century, botanists and gardeners alike have debated whether Romanesco is a broccoli or cauliflower. Its exotic-looking heads taste more like broccoli than cauliflower and are tender like broccoli. But plants are much taller than the usual broccoli, over 3 feet, and don't produce any shoots after the main head is cut. The debate continues. Romanesco grows best in northern climates or in late fall in the South.

(85 Days)

Chapter Four

Carrots

Historical, unusual, and highly colored—these are the best adjectives to describe crunchy, sweet carrots. It's difficult to find another vegetable with such a storied past and unusual uses. One interesting folk story that carrots improve night vision enabled the British Royal Air Force (RAF) in 1940 to disguise its use of radar from the Germans. The RAF boasted that the accuracy of its fighter pilots at night was the result of them eating large amounts of carrots. The Germans bought the story, as it was part of their folklore, too, and began bombing only at night, when the British had the advantage of radar.

The first carrots came from Afghanistan in 900 A.D. and were purple. Their roots were forked, thin, and fibrous—too tough to eat. Gradually the roots mutated, turning yellow and a pale orange. And, they became edible. The Afghan hill people, who were sun-worshippers, believed eating anything yellow or orange inspired a sense of righteousness. People also ate yellow and purple conical taproot varieties of carrots in Pakistan. Arab merchants traveling the trade routes of Africa, Arabia, and Asia took seeds of the purple carrot to Africa and Asia with them. From North Africa, the Moors brought the Afghani purple carrot to Spain and the rest of Europe. The Emperor Caligula (37-51 A.D.), a renowned crazed megalomaniac, attempted to make his horse Incitatus an advisor. He fed the entire Roman Senate a banquet only of carrot dishes, believing their purported aphrodisiac powers would make the Senators see the horse as an alluring, wise friend. Modern carrots arrived in America with the Jamestown settlers who planted them between rows of tobacco.

Over time, the carrots lost their anthocyanins, the compounds that gave them their purple and red tones. Today's deep orange colored, sweet carrots came from breeding done by the famous French seed house of Vilmorin in the last half of the 1800s. But now carrots come in white, purple, black, orange, red, and yellow colors. They are such an important part of the American diet that they provide nearly 30 percent of a person's daily vitamin A consumption.

In the Kitchen with Doreen

Carrots

Rinse and scrub carrots instead of peeling them; most of the nutrients and flavor are just below the surface. The roots are high in carotene (a source of vitamin A), potassium, calcium, and phosphorous, yet low in calories despite their high sugar content.

Use white carrots in soups and stews because they keep their spicy flavor throughout long periods of cooking.

Roman banquets often featured raw carrots, shredded and dressed with oil, salt, and vinegar. Cooked carrots topped with a sauce made from cumin, salt, stale wine, and oil was another favorite. Both dishes are tasty, fast to prepare, and epicurean additions to any meal today. Try topping grilled salmon with the shredded carrot mix.

Don't store harvested carrots near apples or other fruits that give off ethylene gas. The carrots will taste bitter.

Remove carrot tops before storing them in the refrigerator. The greens drain the carrots of moisture, making them limp and dry.

Don't throw away the carrot greens after you remove them—they are high in vitamin K. Dice them and add to soups, stews, and stir-fries for the vitamin boost and a mild carrot-parsley flavor.

For salads and edible accents, make carrot curls by slicing them with a potato peeler. Drop the curls into a bowl of ice water to crisp them and tighten the curls.

Tropical Carrot Relish

Makes 6 servings

½ cup golden raisins
2 pounds carrots, unpeeled
3 tablespoons sugar
3 tablespoons freshly squeezed
    lemon juice, plus additional
    to taste
¼ cup sour cream
⅓ cup mayonnaise
1 tablespoon kosher salt, plus
    additional to taste
1½ teaspoons freshly ground
    pepper
1 cup diced golden pineapple

Place the raisins in a small bowl and add enough hot tap water to cover.

Fit a food processor with the coarsest grating disk. Wash the carrots and cut them to fit in the feed tube of the food processor, lying on their sides. Grate the carrots and put them in a large bowl. Sprinkle the carrots with the sugar and lemon juice.

In a smaller bowl, whisk together the sour cream, mayonnaise, salt, and pepper. Add this mixture and the pineapple to the carrots and toss well. Drain the raisins and add to the salad. Toss the salad. Cover with plastic wrap and chill for 1 hour, if possible, to allow the flavors to blend. Add additional salt and lemon juice, if desired, and serve cold or at room temperature.

Mustard-Glazed Carrots

Makes 6 servings

2 pounds carrots, peeled and cut
    on the diagonal into ¼-inch-
    thick slices
½ cup water
3 tablespoons butter
3 tablespoons Dijon mustard
2 tablespoons brown sugar
Chopped flat-leaf parsley

Add the carrots and water to a large pot and bring to a boil over high heat. Cover, reduce the heat to medium, and cook for about 10 minutes, until crisp-tender. Drain well. Return the carrots to the pot and stir in the butter, mustard, and sugar. Cook over medium heat, stirring, for 1 to 2 minutes, until the carrots are glazed. Sprinkle with parsley and serve.

Carrot

Red Core Chantenay

One of the sweetest carrots you can grow, Red Core Chantenay is crisp, yet tender with an enjoyable mouth-feel. A European import from the 1800s, it has deep red-orange color to the core, is cone-shaped with broad shoulders, and is 5 to 7 inches long. Red Core Chantenay grows well in heavy clay soils and sweetens in storage, even in the cold ground over winter if it's properly mulched.

(60 to 75 Days)

Belgium White

Belgium White has a spicy, hearty flavor that holds up well in cooking. First documented in 1863, Belgium White grows anywhere, even in poor soils, and is productive. Its roots are 8 to 10 inches long but it's not cold hardy, so harvest before the first frost and store indoors.

(60 to 75 Days)

Oxheart

Oxheart has more carrot flavor than most varieties, but it's not as sweet. The heart-shaped, stubby roots are 5 to 6 inches long, 5 inches in diameter, and can weigh up 1 pound each. Easy to pull out of the ground, due to its shape and heft, Oxheart is an excellent storage carrot for northern gardeners. It was first mentioned in seed catalogs in 1884.

(70 to 80 Days)

Danvers

Crisp with a mild flavor, this carrot is also called Danvers 126 and Danvers Half Long. First grown by market gardeners near Danvers, Massachusetts, in the 1870s, its deep orange 6- to 8-inch roots are nearly coreless. Danvers grows in any soil type, is a prolific producer, and stores well.

(75 Days)

Carrot

Parisian Rondo

Parisian Rondo was the standard market carrot during the 1800s due to its intensely sweet flavor and ability to grow in heavy soil or in greenhouses. Its small, round roots are 1 to 2 inches in diameter and red-orange to the core. Parisian Rondo can easily be grown in containers that are at least 6 inches deep.

(65 to 75 Days)

Carrot

Purple Dragon

Purple Dragon has a sweet, spicy flavor that stands up well when cooked. If eaten raw, it has a hint of rosemary and juniper flavors. Add a dash of lemon juice or rind and a couple drops of honey when cooking purple carrots to bring out the spiciness. Purple Dragon is 5 to 6 inches long with a snubbed tip; a purple exterior surrounds a dark orange center. A Class III heirloom bred by Dr. John Navazio from an ancient Chinese purple carrot in the mid-1990s, he named it Dragon, but people quickly called it that "Purple Dragon" carrot. Highly nutritious, even for a carrot, Purple Dragon contains as much antioxidants and lycopene as tomatoes. This variety stores in the cold ground well.

(65 Days)

Chapter Five

Corn

Maize, as corn is called in most of the world, was domesticated in the highlands of southern Mexico about 2,000 B.C. by local tribes, and quickly became a staple food along with beans and squash. That trio is referred to as the "Three Sisters" and, when grown together, each provides nutrients or support for one another. Corn has many ritual uses for native peoples. Various kernel colors are selected for ceremonies and feast foods, and pollen is collected for ceremonial and medicinal purposes. To this day, the Tarahumara Indians in northern Mexico drink a weak beer called tiswin, made by fermenting corn kernels, to bring on stupors or trances for spiritual purposes.

This New World vegetable saved the first colonists at Jamestown from starving. The Pueblo Indians of the American Southwest were raising irrigated corn when Coronado arrived in 1540. Corn then spread north and east to other Indian tribes, and by the time Europeans arrived, corn was a diet staple. The Jamestown settlers would have starved had it not been for the Native Americans who gave them corn seeds and taught the hungry pioneers how to grow it.

Both man and nature have selected traits that are classified by the characteristics of a specific corn's kernels. Flint corn is mostly hard with smooth, hard seeds. Dried, flint stores the best. Flour corn is soft and starchy with thin seed coats. It's best for grinding into cornmeal and flour. Dent corn has hard, flinty sides with soft starchy cores whose kernel ends collapse or "dent" when it's dried. Dent varieties are the most widely grown in the U.S. and are used for oil, syrup, grits, meal, and flour. Sweet corn skins are thin and its kernels are soft and sweet; it is mainly for fresh consumption.

Corn quickly became a staple of the American diet. By 1900, American ingenuity produced the first processed or shelf-stable corn product—corn flakes. In little Battle Creek, Michigan, a huge industry was created to produce corn flakes, which consumers couldn't get enough of. There were forty-four cereal companies specializing in cornflakes, including the surviving brands Kellogg's and Post.

In the Kitchen with Doreen

Corn

Pick fresh corn at the "milk" stage for the best flavor and maximum sweetness. Pierce a kernel in the middle of a cob with your fingernail or a knife tip; if milky juice (or even clear liquid) flows, it's perfect to eat. As corn dries, it becomes tougher and loses its sweetness.

Use a damp paper towel to quickly remove corn silks; silks readily adhere to the moist paper. Wipe downward towards the cob's tip.

Red sweet corn provides 20 percent more protein than white corn or yellow corn. And it contains 350 percent more antioxidants, including anthocyanin, the pigment that creates the red color in this corn.

Add flavor to roasted corn by topping an ear with a sprig of marjoram before you wrap it in foil for grilling.

Corn smut is a black, bulbous fungus that causes corn kernels to swell to many times their size. The Aztecs considered it a delicacy, and it is still prized in Mexican cuisine. James Beard called it Mexican "truffles." It's also called huitlacoche and has a sweet, smoky flavor. Look for it in gourmet markets fresh, canned, and frozen.

Steam freshly picked ears of corn, rather than boiling them, for the best flavor. Any ears you don't eat can be frozen.

Cut off the kernels from five ears of steamed corn and toss them with lime juice, a drizzle of olive oil, and minced chives and cilantro or parsley to make a corn relish. Top grilled chicken breasts or fish fillets with a couple of tablespoons of this relish for a fresh, trendy summer dish.

Sautéed Corn on the Cob with Chili-Lime-Cilantro Spread

Makes 4 servings

4 ears corn, shucked
½ cup light sour cream
4 teaspoons finely chopped fresh cilantro
2 teaspoons chili powder
½ teaspoon garlic powder or 1 clove garlic, finely chopped
1 teaspoon freshly squeezed lime juice
Salt
Freshly ground pepper
2 tablespoons butter

Place the corn on a microwavable plate and cover tightly with plastic wrap. Microwave on high until the corn is fully cooked, 8 to 10 minutes. (The corn can be prepared up to 2 hours ahead.)

In a small bowl, mix the sour cream, cilantro, chili powder, garlic, lime juice, salt, and pepper. Cover and chill until ready to serve.

About 10 minutes before serving, heat the butter in a skillet over medium to medium-high heat. Add the corn and cook, turning with kitchen tongs every few minutes, until golden brown, about 6 minutes. Serve immediately, with the sour cream spread in a separate bowl.

Confetti Corn

Makes 6 servings

2 tablespoons extra-virgin olive oil
⅓ cup chopped red onion
1 small orange bell pepper, ½-inch diced
2 tablespoons unsalted butter
Kernels cut from 5 ears corn (4 cups)
1½ teaspoons kosher salt, plus additional to taste
1 teaspoon freshly ground pepper, plus additional to taste
2 tablespoons minced fresh chives

Heat the oil in a large skillet over medium heat. Add the onion and sauté for 5 minutes, until the onion is soft. Stir in the bell pepper and sauté for 2 more minutes.

Add the butter to the pan and allow it to melt. Over medium heat, add the corn, salt, and pepper and cook, stirring occasionally, for 5 to 7 minutes, until the corn just loses its starchiness. Season with salt and pepper, gently stir in the chives, and serve hot.

Sweet

Blue Jade

Blue Jade is blue, extra sweet (without the sugar enhancement of a hybrid), and miniature. How cool is that? This heirloom is the *only* sweet corn that can be grown in containers. Plants grow only to about 30 inches and bear 3- to 6-inch-long, steel-blue ears that turn jade-blue when they're boiled. Pick ears immediately prior to eating so their sugar content is the highest possible (the sugars in corn convert to starches over time). Blue Jade makes a colorful and tasty creamed corn that freezes very well.

(70 to 80 Days)

Golden Bantam

This heirloom produces two small ears per plant with robust sweetness. Short—5 feet tall or less—it tolerates poor growing conditions and still produces. A farmer named William Chambers of Greenfield, Massachusetts, grew this corn for years. After he died, a friend sold some of Chambers' seeds to W. Atlee Burpee, who featured it in his 1902 seed catalog and selected its name to match the corn's size. When it was introduced, Burpee was taking a big chance, because yellow kernel corn was thought of as horse feed. Gardeners preferred white corn to grow for the table. By 1926, Golden Bantam was declared America's favorite sweet corn by Burpee and garden writers.

(75 to 80 Days)

Stowell's Evergreen

Not only is this sweet white corn full of flavor, but you don't have to pick it immediately to get the best quality; it retains its tender sweetness for a long time on the plant. It even keeps indoors if you hang the stalks with ears attached upside-down in a cold, but not freezing, location. Some have reported eating Stowell's Evergreen in January! The stalks are 9 to 10 feet tall and have at least two extra-large ears. One of the oldest cultivated corn varieties still in existence today, Stowell's Evergreen was noted in catalogs in 1856.

(80 to 100 Days)

Guarijio Red

Deep rich red and exceptionally sweet in flavor, Guarijio Red offers a soft, yet firm, texture. Its vivid color deepens when it's cooked. This variety is sensitive to length of day requirements; plant in early June and harvest in October. Occasionally, a yellow ear will turn up with the slender red cobs. Guarijio Red originated in Sonora, Mexico. To store, refrigerate up to five days for optimum quality. If left at room temperature, the red color of the kernels will be absorbed back into the cob.

(110 to 125 Days)

Luther Hill

Extra sweet in taste, this heirloom white corn is still used by breeders for its flavor genes to create hybrid sweet corn varieties. In fact, Luther Hill is one of the parental lines of Silver Queen hybrid sweet corn. Bred in 1902 in Andover Township, New Jersey, by Rutgers University horticulturist Luther Hill, seeds produce two 6-inch ears on 4- to 6-foot-tall stalks with some suckers. This small corn is adapted to the Appalachian foothills and grows best in cooler climates—even as far north as Canada.

(70 to 85 Days)

Sweet

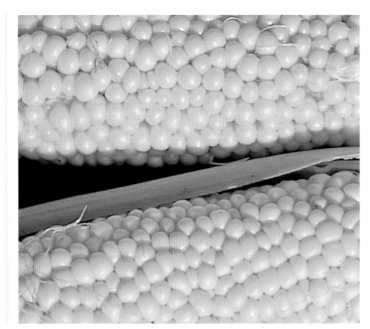

Country Gentleman

A sweet, tender, and robustly flavored white corn, Country Gentleman is still a popular farm market crop that was introduced in 1890 by S.D. Woodruff & Sons. The ears have no rows, as it is a shoe peg type, and small narrow kernels are packed in a zigzag pattern. Nine-foot-tall stalks usually set two ears that are 8 inches long. You can tell when pollination is complete because its silks turn a brilliant red.

(80 to 100 Days)

Black Aztec

Sweet, tender, and juicy when picked at the milk stage, Black Aztec's white kernels turn a deep black-blue as they mature. They can be ground for corn flour and make colorful and delicious cornbread and tortillas. Sometimes called Black Mexican, Black Aztec was first offered in seed catalogs as Black Mexican in 1864. It's believed to have its origins in New York, possibly grown by the Iroquois. This hardy corn grows in almost any climate, and its 6-foot-tall stalks produce large ears that are 7 inches long or longer.

(65 to 85 Days)

Flour, Flint, and Dent

Hopi Blue

Hopi Blue is a soft, grinding corn used for cornmeal, roasting corn, tamales, and hominy. Besides being the backbone of their diet, blue corn represents an essential part of the Hopi culture. It symbolizes the rising sun, the beginning of life, wisdom, and understanding. This heirloom flint corn is still a staple of the Hopi Indians in northern Arizona. Bushy, 5-foot-tall stalks yield 8- to 10-inch ears with smooth blue kernels.

(75 to 110 Days)

Flour, Flint, and Dent

Wachichu Flint

Wachichu Flint is a Native American heirloom that can be eaten fresh, roasted, or ground into flour. Slender ears almost a foot long exhibit an enormous range of colors and patterns. Plants are large, topping out at over 9 feet. When dried, the kernels have a hard, translucent seed coat. These vigorous, bushy plants make an effective windbreak or an excellent livestock forage. It tolerates cool soils.

(90 to 105 Days)

Bloody Butcher

Full of sweet, corny flavor when it's picked young, Bloody Butcher is also good for flour or cornmeal. This colorful heirloom dates to the early 1800s when it originated by mixing Native American corn with white corn seed. The 10- to 12-foot-tall stalks each hold two to six ears of blood red kernels striped with a darker red; the cobs are either pink or red. This variety needs a long growing season but it is drought tolerant.

(100-120 Days)

Flour, Flint, and Dent

Anasazi

Anasazi can be eaten as a sweet corn if the ears are picked early; the flavor is intense, sweet, and enjoyable. This is a rare heirloom variety whose seed, from samples found in a cave in Utah, has been carbon dated to 800 years old. Its multicolored kernels contain every color found in native corns with many patterns. Anasazi produces multiple ears on 6- to 9-foot-tall stalks.

(90 to 100 Days)

Tarahumara Maize Colorado

Pick Tarahumara Maize Colorado when it's young for chewy and tasty fresh-roasted corn. It is excellent ground into flour or meal. Tarahumara Maize Colorado is beautiful with a mix of blue, white, purple, and red kernels on the same cob or as single-color cobs. One plant can even have a purple and a red ear!

(Variable on weather; Approx. 120 Days)

Chapter Six

Cucumbers

More than 10,000 years ago, wild cucumbers grew everywhere, but early hunter-gatherer tribes wouldn't eat them. The intensely bitter turpentine taste of wild cucumbers, which is a turpentine resin derivative called *cucurbitacin*, drove hungry people away. It wasn't until 3,000 years later that the cucumber mutated enough to lose much of its cucurbitacin concentration.

Cucumbers were cultivated for at least 3,000 years in Western Asia and migrated to Europe via Roman invasions. The Romans liked cucumbers so much that they grew them in rudimentary greenhouses during winter in the northern empires they conquered. Emperor Tiberius grew cucumbers in carts and had his slaves wheel them around to catch the sun. The story goes that cucumbers were brought to the Americas by Christopher Columbus.

Members of the gourd family, cucumbers are 95 percent water yet they contain most of the vitamins you need daily. One cucumber has vitamin B1, vitamin B2, vitamin B3, vitamin B5, vitamin B6, folic acid, vitamin C, calcium, iron, magnesium, phosphorus, potassium, and zinc.

Pickling and brining have long been ways to preserve food. In India, they discovered that brining cucumbers improved their taste. The Greeks added fresh, acidic yogurt and herbs on top of cucumber slices to keep them fresh for a couple of days; Asians used rice vinegar to preserve cucumbers; Europeans pickled everything from cucumbers and green beans to sweet peppers and meat. With this cultural history, it's no wonder that a huge pickling industry developed in the United States.

When the Industrial Revolution sent families to cities for jobs, Henry J. Heinz started bottling and selling pickles. He delivered a product that new city wives didn't have the time or materials to make. Heinz started making pickles in 1876, and by 1888 had a 22-acre factory complex in Pittsburgh. Commercially bottled pickles became so popular that in 1884, *Good Housekeeping* magazine stated, "A dinner or lunch without pickles of some kind is incomplete." Consumption rose to almost 10 pounds per person by the time Heinz died in 1919. We are still a pickle-crazed country—more than 26 billion pickles are sold every year.

In the Kitchen with Doreen

Cucumbers

Eat a cucumber to tame the burn from hot peppers like jalapeño. It will immediately neutralize the capsicum of the pepper that causes the burning in your mouth. Cucumbers fight bad breath too. Press a slice or two to the roof of your mouth with your tongue and hold for 30 seconds. The phytochemicals in cucumbers will kill the bacteria responsible for causing bad breath.

Cucumbers are best when they're used fresh, but if a cucumber is a little wilted, soaking it in salted ice water for 1 to 2 hours will restore its crispness.

This is my favorite, fast cucumber salad recipe: Slice cucumbers thin; combine ⅓ cup rice wine vinegar and 1 teaspoon sugar; and pour over slices. Top with chopped fresh cilantro, and black or white toasted sesame seeds. Refrigerate 30 minutes or more before serving.

Cut cucumbers in half lengthwise, scoop out the seeds, and then cut them into ¼-inch chunks for stir-fry dishes. They add crispness and absorb the flavors of other ingredients, such as shrimp or lemongrass.

"Cool as a cucumber" isn't just an old-fashioned saying. Cool down by eating a few slices; a cucumber is about 20 degrees cooler than the surrounding air.

Eaten raw, cucumbers have the same enzyme, called erepsin, as papayas do. Erepsin is a powerful protein-digesting compound. So include cucumbers with that big steak dinner.

Combine equal amounts of chopped cucumbers, cantaloupe, and watermelon for a scrumptious summer salad. Sprinkle with fresh mint leaves, toss, and serve. Fruity mint varieties like Pineapple, Orange, or Banana make the salad taste even better!

Cucumber and Watermelon Salad

Makes 4 servings

3 cups peeled and ½-inch cubed
    English cucumber
3 cups ½-inch cubed seedless watermelon
3 tablespoons fresh lime juice
¾ teaspoon kosher salt
⅛ teaspoon freshly ground pepper

In a large bowl, toss the cucumber and watermelon with the lime juice, salt, and pepper. Serve immediately.

Tomato and Cucumber Salad

Makes 8 servings

4 tomatoes, cored and cut into 8 wedges
2 peeled cucumbers, cut in half lengthwise
    and then cut into chunks
½ red onion, very thinly sliced
Juice of 1 lemon
2 tablespoons red wine vinegar
4 tablespoons olive oil
¼ cup mint leaves, cut into thin strips
½ teaspoon salt
Several grinds of pepper

Toss all the ingredients together in a large bowl. Taste and adjust seasonings as necessary.

Kool-Aid Pickles

2 packages of your favorite flavor of
    Kool-Aid (the "hotter" the color, the
    more colorful the pickles)
Sugar
Cucumbers, peeled and sliced lengthwise

Make a jar of double-strength Kool-Aid (using the amount of water needed for one package), adding a bit of extra sugar. In a tall jar, arrange the cucumbers, pour the Kool-Aid mixture over them, and refrigerate for a week. Kids love them!

Cucumber

Boothby's Blond

The intense first bite of melon with a dash of honey, plus a crisp, clean finish make Boothby's Blond the best-tasting cucumber I've *ever* eaten. Its skin is tender and sweet too. The creamy yellow color punctuated with black spines makes it a visual treat. Introduced by the Boothby family of Maine in the early 1900s, this cucumber makes high quality pickles. Pick at 4 inches long for the best results.

(60 to 65 Days)

Crystal Apple

Often mistaken for Lemon, another heirloom cucumber that's round and light yellow, Crystal Apple has a light refreshing taste, and tender, creamy skin. It was brought to the United States in 1930 from New Zealand. Its apple-shaped cucumbers are about 3 inches in diameter at their prime. Plants are very productive; pick fruit small for the best quality.

(65 Days)

Cucumber

Boston Pickling

Crunchy and cool in taste, this American heirloom from 1880 provides a continual supply of 2- to 3-inch-long blocky cucumbers for pickling. Boston Pickling's vines are vigorous and productive and are naturally resistant to mosaic virus and cucumber scale, the two diseases that plague all cucumbers.

(57 Days)

Chinese Yellow

Edible and delicious in all stages, Chinese Yellow has apple-crisp white flesh with subtle hints of lemony flavor when it's fully ripened. Chinese Yellow comes from mainland China where it has been grown for centuries. This cucumber is green when it is young, but transforms into an oval shape that has beautiful, striking lemon-orange variegated (non-bitter) skin. When this variety ripens, its stripes fade.

(55 to 60 Days)

A & C Pickling

A & C Pickling's mild melon-y flavor makes this cucumber great in salads and for pickling. Introduced by Abbot & Cobb of Philadelphia in 1928, this heirloom is a heavy producer of uniformly straight, dark green fruit that hold their color in storage. Ripe cucumbers are about 8 to 10 inches long.

(55 Days)

Cucumber

Delikatesse

Not a subtle cucumber, Delikatesse's first bite is full of intense citrusy sweetness that trails to a dash of salt with honey. It's excellent for salads and for making large brined pickles. A rare variety from Germany, Delikatesse is about 10 inches long and lime green with small white warts.

(60 Days)

Japanese Climbing

Refreshing, with an intense melon aftertaste is the only way to describe the exquisite flavor of the Japanese Climbing. The light green, 9-inch-long slicing cucumbers came from Japan in 1892. It's a high-yielding variety best grown on a fence or trellis due to its vigorous vines. This one makes good pickles too.

(58 Days)

Double Yield

A honeyed, melon taste is pervasive in every bite. Double Yield was developed by a home gardener and introduced in 1924. For every cucumber harvested, two or three more form, so keep picking all season. Pick when the fruit is about 4 inches long for the best quality. This heirloom also makes excellent pickles.

(50 Days)

Lemon

Sweeter than other cucumbers, Lemon is never bitter because it lacks the cucurbitacin compounds that make some cucumbers taste acrid. Both the flesh and its numerous, large seeds are firm and tasty. Its thin skin adds crunch and flavor to the ivory, verging on yellow, fruit. It's easy to mistake it for a lemon. Pick Lemon at golfball-size for the best quality. Lemon was introduced to the United States from Australia in 1894.

(65 to 70 Days)

Long Green Improved

A crunchy, slightly sweet first bite with intense melon tones describes Long Green Improved. The 12-inch plump fruit are perfect for slicing and brining when they're mature, and, pickling when they're harvested small. The flesh is firm with few seeds. It was introduced by D. M. Ferry & Co. in 1872, most likely as Ferry's Improved Long Green.

(60 Days)

Cucumber

Longfellow

Cool, crunchy with a hint of lemon, Longfellow grows 12 to 15 inches long, living up to its name. The slender and round-ended fruits are dotted with white spines and are a uniform dark green. It excels as a slicing cucumber. Longfellow was introduced to the seed trade in 1927.

(60 to 75 Days)

Marketer

Marketer's crunchy, fresh taste is accentuated by a hint of salt. An old commercial variety, Marketer was introduced in 1942 and was one of the first All-America Selections in 1943. The 9-inch-long, smooth cucumbers are "burpless," meaning they have no cucurbitacin compounds that create bitterness and digestive problems. It's naturally resistant to powdery mildew and grows in any climate.

(45 to 50 Days)

Cucumber

Parisian Pickling

When picked large for slicing, Parisian Pickling has a cleansing, slightly acidic flavor that holds up well to vinaigrettes. This old French heirloom from 1892 is usually picked small, at about 50 days after planting for gherkins or cornichons. It is known in Europe as Ameliore de Bourbonne.

(50 to 80 Days)

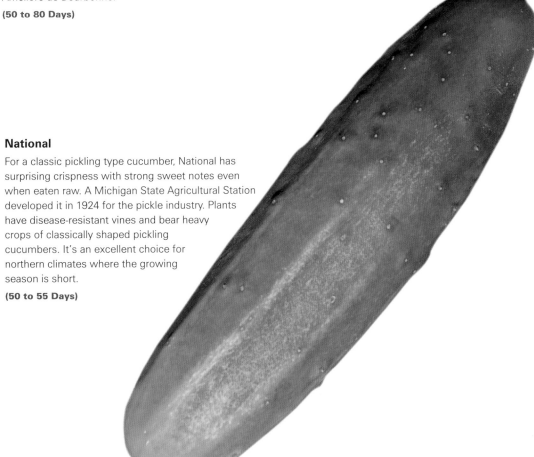

National

For a classic pickling type cucumber, National has surprising crispness with strong sweet notes even when eaten raw. A Michigan State Agricultural Station developed it in 1924 for the pickle industry. Plants have disease-resistant vines and bear heavy crops of classically shaped pickling cucumbers. It's an excellent choice for northern climates where the growing season is short.

(50 to 55 Days)

Cucumber

Snow's Fancy Pickling

Sweet and crisp when eaten raw, this heirloom also makes outstanding pickles. It was selected by J.C. Snow at his famous Snow Pickle Farm in Rockford, Illinois, and introduced in 1905 by Vaughan's Seed House of Chicago. At the time, Snow's Fancy Pickling fit all the requirements for small pickle manufacturing. Plants produce substantial crops of 5-inch-long, narrow pickling cucumbers.

(50 Days)

Cucumber

Ruby Wallace's Old Time White

Don't pick this white cucumber too late! When the skin yellows, its bitterness is pervasive and Ruby Wallace's Old Time White is inedible. When picked small for pickles, the flavor is refreshing with a hint of lemon. It was grown for over fifty years by Mrs. Ruby Wallace of Dallas, North Carolina. Ruby first got a start from her mother-in-law Myrtle, who grew these cucumbers for many years before that. The Wallace family uses the fruits for pickles when they are very small. (Be sure to use white vinegar when making white pickles!)

(50 Days)

Cucumber

Suyo Long

Fresh, crisp, with a slight lemon aftertaste, this ancient Chinese variety is burpless (no cucurbitacin compounds). Train vines to a trellis for straight fruit, because Suyo Long can grow up to 18 inches. It's an excellent slicer and makes tasty bread-and-butter pickles. Suyo Long grows well in any climate, even in hot weather, and sets fruit early.

(60 Days)

Cucumber

White Wonder

White Wonder's fruits are a gorgeous ivory when they're at the perfect slicing stage and are packed with full-bodied, citrusy-sweet flavor. When it turns yellow, White Wonder is past its prime and flavor diminishes dramatically. Introduced by the W. Atlee Burpee Seed Company in 1893, this heirloom produces large crops even during hot weather.

(60 Days)

Chapter Seven

Eggplants

Whether they're called *aubergine, berengina, patlican,* or *melenzane,* eggplants got their name because they were only one color in the wild—white—and they looked like hen's eggs hanging from thorny plants. Eggplants are native to India and modern day Pakistan, and were first domesticated there over 4,000 years ago. They were called *melongena,* which means "eggplant" in Sanskrit. The large black-purple-fruited eggplant we know today was the first to be domesticated. It, along with the white egg types, spread into neighboring China about 500 B.C. and became a culinary favorite to generations of Chinese emperors. Centuries ago, affluent Chinese ladies used black eggplant skins to fashionably stain their teeth.

Eggplant traveled to Europe courtesy of the Moor invasion in the sixth century and became known as *aubergine* from the French word that translates as "like a peach." In India and medieval Europe, eggplant was credited with remarkable properties as a love potion.

Botanically, eggplants are related to tomatoes (and potatoes), and are members of the nightshade family. By the 1600s, northern Europeans were calling eggplants "mad apples" in the belief that eating them caused insanity (a description also applied to tomatoes). How quickly love turned to crazy! Several decades later, the French brought eggplant to the dinner table, and it finally found favor as a vegetable. Thomas Jefferson, ever the experimental botanist, introduced eggplant to the United States as an ornamental. Although most Americans didn't eat eggplants until the Great Depression, eggplant stuffed with onion, breadcrumbs, tomatoes, and celery is said to have been one of President Andrew Johnson's favorite dishes.

Often called a "fat sponge" for its ability to soak up vast amounts of cooking oil, eggplant is frequently used for ethnic favorites such as the Italian eggplant Parmesan, which is fried, sauced with marinara, and topped with melted cheese. But there are a plethora of culinary delights such as the Middle Eastern classic appetizer baba ghanoush, roasted eggplant combined with tahini and garlic; Greek moussaka, a layered casserole of eggplant, ground lamb, and béchemel sauce; and the French ratatouille, a stew of eggplant, tomatoes, garlic, zucchini, bell peppers, and onion. No matter what you call it, it's all delicious!

In the Kitchen with Doreen

Eggplants

White-skinned varieties are not bitter like the black-skinned ones. Pink and pale purple eggplants are considered white skinned because that is the color of their undercoat. These pale varieties are great for grilling on the barbecue or for fresh relishes. There is no need to salt and allow bitter juices to drain away like you have to do with Black Beauty and other black-skinned eggplants.

To keep eggplants from turning brown after you peel them, sprinkle with lemon juice or soak in water with lemon juice added.

Stuff small eggplants with savory fillings such as cooked Italian sausage and garlic breadcrumbs, topped with Romano or Asiago cheese. Bake until the tops are browned.

Another fast and tasty eggplant dish, traditional in China, is baby eggplant stir-fried with bean sprouts, peppers, and tomatoes. Drizzle with sesame seed oil, sprinkle with chopped cilantro, and serve.

Diced eggplant with cured olives, pepperoncini, and tomatoes create a spicy relish that adds flavor to any dish from sandwiches to pasta.

Roast a halved eggplant, scoop out the cooked flesh, mash it, and combine with roasted garlic, grated Parmesan cheese, and chopped porcini mushrooms for a gourmet side dish that will put mashed potatoes to shame.

Never eat or serve eggplant raw because it contains the same toxic compound, solanine, found in green potatoes.

Take advantage of eggplant's low calorie count and use slices of it instead of lasagna noodles.

Hearty Eggplant Ragout

Makes 4 to 6 servings

1 to 1½ pounds Ping Tung Long eggplant
Salt
Freshly ground pepper
6 tablespoons olive oil, divided
1 large onion, ½-inch diced
1 large Jimmy Nardello or Italian frying
    peppers, cut into strips
2 zucchini, cut into 1-inch-thick rounds
1 teaspoon paprika
½ teaspoon turmeric
2 cloves garlic, finely chopped
2 tablespoons tomato paste
1½ cups or more tomato chunks, peeled and
    seeded first, any juices reserved
1 (15-ounce) can chickpeas, drained
8 sprigs fresh cilantro, chopped
8 sprigs fresh flat-leaf parsley, chopped
Harissa, for serving

Cut the eggplant into large chunks. Sprinkle with salt and pepper and set aside for 30 minutes to release the juices. Rinse quickly and pat dry.

Heat 4 tablespoons of the oil in a large skillet over high heat until hazy. Add the eggplant and stir quickly. Reduce the heat to medium and cook, turning the pieces every few minutes, until golden, about 10 minutes. Remove from the heat.

Warm the remaining 2 tablespoons of oil in a Dutch oven over medium-high heat. Add the onion, peppers, and zucchini and cook until the onion is lightly browned around the edges, 8 to 10 minutes. Toward the end, add the paprika, turmeric, and garlic, taking care not to burn the garlic. Stir in the tomato paste, then moisten the pot with a few tablespoons of water and scrape off the juices from the bottom. Add the tomatoes, eggplant, chickpeas, 1½ cups water, and 1 teaspoon salt. Reduce the heat to a simmer, cover, and cook for 20 minutes, stirring once or twice. Stir in the cilantro and parsley. Serve with the harissa.

Eggplant Spread

Makes 6 servings

1 medium eggplant, peeled and cubed
2 red bell peppers, seeded and diced
1 red onion, peeled and diced
2 garlic cloves, minced
3 tablespoons olive oil
1 ½ teaspoons salt
½ teaspoon freshly ground pepper
1 tablespoon tomato paste

Preheat the oven to 400 degrees F. Combine the eggplant, peppers, and onion in a large bowl. Toss with the garlic, olive oil, salt, and pepper. Spread on a baking sheet and roast 45 minutes, or until the vegetables are lightly brown and softened, turning once during roasting. Cool.

In a food processor, pulse the cooled vegetables with the tomato paste to blend. Season again with the salt and pepper. Serve with toasted pita wedges.

Eggplant

Black Beauty

This 1902 Italian import is what most people think of as an eggplant—a purple-black, large, teardrop-shaped fruit. Full of subtle flavors, Black Beauty is famous for soaking up tomato-based sauces and for frying crisply. Each fruit can weigh up to 3 pounds, and a plant will produce six or more of them. Also called Imperial Black Beauty, this heirloom grows better in cooler climates than most eggplants do.

(75 to 90 Days)

Rosa Bianca

A stunning Italian heirloom—it has white skin streaked with lavender—the meaty fruits have a creamy consistency and delicate, sweet flavor. Prized by chefs, Rosa Bianca is good for roasting, frying, and grilling. Heavy-yielding plants need warmth and should be protected in cooler climates.

(75 to 90 Days)

Eggplant

Turkish Orange

The orange fruits of Turkish Orange explode with ambrosial sweetness and fragrance when freshly cut. The size and shape of a Roma-type tomato, fruits start out green, gradually adding wide orange streaks that merge, turning this heirloom solid orange-red at maturity. It is an excellent stuffing eggplant, tender, sweet, and fragrant at the orange-streaked stage. Mature eggplants are tough and bitter, though. Tall plants produce up to fifteen fruits in a season. Originating in Turkey, this gorgeous eggplant found its way to the United States via Italy. It's also called Red Egg.

(65 to 85 Days)

Ping Tung Long

Deep lavender, slender, and with fruits up to 1 foot long, gorgeous Ping Tung Long came from Taiwan (its name is its town of origin) several centuries ago. The shiny fruits are perfect for skewering and grilling. Brush slices with olive oil and garlic to highlight its delicate flavor. Each disease-resistant, vigorous plant produces twenty or more eggplants.

(65 to 75 Days)

Chapter Eight

Lettuces

As each of us munches our way through an annual 34 pounds of lettuce (a six-fold increase since 1900), we should remember that our great-grandparents believed that eating lettuce reduced fertility and spawned children who were crazy. Part of that belief may have come from Elizabethan England, where lettuce, cabbage, spinach, and radishes were considered fit only for the poor or to feed animals.

While the English scorned lettuce, the French candied it in the seventeenth century. They prepared a dessert using lettuce hearts coated with honey. Eventually, they served an entire head at the table for salads, where it became popular in Louis XIV's reign. He liked his lettuce seasoned with tarragon, basil, and violets. Lettuce came to the Americas in 1493 when Columbus planted the vegetable in the West Indies. The first colonists brought seeds with them, and both George Washington and Thomas Jefferson planted lettuce for salads to serve to guests. By 1880 there were over 300 lettuce varieties listed in various seed catalogs—a number that fell dramatically.

In 2000, 73 percent of all lettuce grown in the United States was Iceberg. Tasteless but crisp, pale green Iceberg dominated salad bowls until recently when a new breed of chefs introduced beautiful and tasty heirloom lettuces to the public. The trend to eat more healthily contributed to the acceptance of these "new" lettuces. Baby and leaf lettuce mixes have made rapid inroads in grocery produce sections and offer a full array of colors, flavors, and textures. Lettuce types include *crispheads*, known for their crispy, juicy texture and very mild flavor; *looseleafs*, which are harvested leaf by leaf and resprout vigorously from their stems, making them useful for a continuous harvest; *butterhead* lettuces, whose loose heads have soft, buttery-textured leaves with a mild, sweet, and juicy flavor; and *romaines*, which have a crisp texture, slightly bitter flavor, and high nutritional content.

Nearly all of these lettuces are grown today in California and are available year-round. Most gardeners can't duplicate that feat, but you can grow colorful, tasty heirloom lettuces throughout their growing season or find them at farmers' markets in season.

In the Kitchen with Doreen

Lettuces

Lettuce may become bitter during hot weather or when seed stalks begin to form. Wash and store the leaves in the refrigerator for a day or two; much of the bitterness will disappear.

Don't throw away those outer leaves! The darker green the lettuce leaf is, the more nutrition it has. Romaine leaves Iceberg in the dust, with almost ten times the antioxidants and vitamins.

For a fast Thai wrap, use butterhead lettuce leaves. Lay grilled chicken strips on leaves and top with a mix of freshly chopped mint and cilantro. Combine soy sauce, grated ginger, and sesame oil in a jar and drizzle some of the dressing over the wrap filing. Serve immediately or put the ingredients on the table and let everyone make their own.

Salt lettuce salads just before serving. If they are salted earlier, lettuce leaves wilt and toughen.

Try steaming baby lettuce leaves and early spring peas for a taste sensation.

Lettuces can be refrigerated up to three days without loss of nutrients or quality. Line the vegetable crisper with paper towels to absorb any excess water and keep leaves crisp.

Leaves and heads shouldn't be washed until they're used, as excess water will wilt them. After washing, blot with paper towels or use a salad spinner to remove moisture.

You should tear lettuce leaves rather than cut them. *Not true!* This is an old wives' tale. Lettuce leaves won't turn brown if you slice them with a knife.

Green Salad with Vinaigrette

Makes 6 to 8 servings

3 tablespoons champagne vinegar or white wine vinegar
½ teaspoon Dijon mustard
½ teaspoon minced garlic
1 egg yolk, at room temperature
¾ teaspoon kosher salt
¼ teaspoon freshly ground pepper
½ cup extra-virgin olive oil
Salad greens or mesclun mix for 6 to 8 people
½ cup crumbled feta cheese

In a small bowl, whisk together the vinegar, mustard, garlic, egg yolk, salt, and pepper. While whisking, slowly add the oil until the vinaigrette is emulsified.

In a large bowl, toss the greens with enough dressing to moisten. Sprinkle the feta cheese over the salad and serve immediately.

Heirloom Lettuce Salad with Onion, Apple, Celery Heart, and Sweet Vinaigrette

Makes 6 servings

½ medium onion, thinly sliced
1 red apple, cored and thinly sliced
1 cup julienned celery hearts (You can purchase celery hearts separately or just use the innermost stalks of celery from a regular bunch.)
Tom Thumb and/or Red Oakleaf lettuce
1 teaspoon Dijon mustard
2 tablespoons red wine vinegar
2 tablespoons lemon juice
1 tablespoon sugar
Salt, to taste
Freshly ground pepper, to taste
3 tablespoons olive oil

Toss the onion, apple, celery hearts, and lettuce (enough for 6 people) together in a large bowl.

In a small bowl, whisk together the mustard, vinegar, lemon juice, sugar, salt, and pepper. While whisking, slowly add the oil until the vinaigrette is emulsified. Add the vinaigrette to the salad and toss.

Looseleaf

Red Oak Leaf

Red Oak Leaf has the same crisp sweetness as Green Oak Leaf, but dark burgundy leaf color sets it apart. It colors deeply in full sun and doesn't turn bitter. Due to its color, this heirloom is ignored by slugs and snails. The red pigment in the leaves is full of compounds that can prevent heart disease.

(50 to 70 Days)

Green Oak Leaf

This heirloom, first mentioned in 1686, provides plenty of crisp, lightly sweet and nutty, deeply lobed for leaves for most of the spring and summer. Green Oak Leaf is very heat tolerant and forms tall, tight rosettes of deep green leaves. Its leaves should be harvested from the outer rings.

(40 to 60 Days)

Prizehead

Crunchy and sweet, but with a trace of bitter counter note, is the most accurate description of Prizehead's sophisticated flavor. This heirloom lettuce is still winning prizes for that taste and its curled leaves of light green with pinkish tips. It is a standout in the garden and on the table for the brightness of its contrasting colors. Nonheading, despite the misleading name, Prizehead is fast growing and does best in cooler weather. It was listed in seed catalogs before 1920.

(45 to 50 Days)

Looseleaf

Black-Seeded Simpson

Crisp, juicy, with a trace of sweetness, this popular heirloom from 1850 is still widely planted. Leaves are large, crinkly, light green, and never turn bitter. Heat, drought, and cold tolerant, this reliable leaf lettuce can be planted through early summer for a continuous supply.

(40 to 55 Days)

Deer Tongue

Deer Tongue's tender, robustly flavored leaves tolerate heat and cold. Its slightly savoyed, triangular green leaves grow in a rosette around a loose head. You can also find this nineteenth century heirloom under the names Matchless and Rodin.

(45 to 70 Days)

Lollo Rosa

Mildly sweet with subtle crisp texture, Lollo Rosa's Bordeaux-red-edged leaves are deeply frilled and curled. It's an excellent baby lettuce harvested early or as a cut-and-come-again type. Harvest mature rosettes of about 8 inches in diameter two months after planting, as they aren't heat tolerant. An heirloom from Italy, Lollo Rosa is still the most popular leaf lettuce there and throughout Europe.

(30 to 55 Days)

Crisphead

Iceberg

Full of crunch and juiciness, this classic crisphead lettuce is perfect for home gardens because of its compact size, crisp heart and disease resistance. Outer leaves are waxy (to repel insects) and are tipped with a bronze fringe. Iceberg lettuce got its name from the fact that California growers started shipping it covered with heaps of crushed ice in the 1920s. Previously, it had been called Crisphead and was first listed in seed catalogs in 1894.

(50 to 85 Days)

Sierra Batavian

This old favorite has a sweet and nutty taste, forming an open head with glossy green leaves veined in coppery red. This heirloom been planted in home gardens since the early 1900s because its flavor remains delicious no matter how hot the weather. Sierra Batavian also forms additional smaller heads once the primary head has been harvested.

(50 to 60 Days)

Hanson

Large, yellowish green heads have attractive, frilly leaves with sweet and juicy white hearts. Hanson's outer leaves are crisp and juicy, but they lack the sweetness of the heart. Unlike some lettuces, this variety tolerates heat. Hanson was the most widely planted lettuce in American gardens in 1904; it dates to 1850. It's also called Hanson Improved.

(65 to 80 Days)

Butterhead (Bibb)

Grandpa Admire's

Grandpa Admire's has a mild, refined flavor. Its thick, buttery leaves are tinged with bronze and form a loose Bibb-type head. This variety resists bolting and doesn't turn bitter. It's named for George Admire, a Civil War veteran, who found the bronzy lettuce in his garden about 1820. His 90-year-old granddaughter, Cloe Lowrey, gave the seeds to Seed Savers Exchange in 1977.

(45 to 60 Days)

Tom Thumb

Sweet, crisp green leaves with a flowery finish and small size make Tom Thumb perfect for a single-serving salad; one 5-inch-diameter plant is just right. It grows well under lights indoors, in greenhouses, and in cold frames. This English heirloom is related to Tennis Ball but is more heat tolerant.

(48 to 55 Days)

Butterhead (Bibb)

Forellenschuss

Not only is Forellenschuss beautiful, but this eye-catching lettuce is a crinkled-leafed savoy type. Smooth, buttery flavor drenches the leaves, which form loose heads 8 to 10 inches wide. This Austrian heirloom, with apple green leaves splattered with claret and brown spots, is also called Speckled Trout and Troutback. Grow it in cool weather and harvest before hot days arrive.

(50 to 65 Days)

Merveille des Quatre Saisons

The gorgeous French heirloom, with cranberry-tipped purplish green outer leaves and tight ivory hearts, is full of sweetness that holds even in hot weather. Its heads are 6 to 10 inches in diameter. It's also called Four Seasons, the English translation of its French name.

(55 to 70 Days)

Butterhead (Bibb)

Tennis Ball

Tennis Ball's flavor is mild and crisp, though not as refined as Tom Thumb. Its light green outer leaves conceal a yellow-green heart. Like Tom Thumb, Tennis Ball is a single-serving size and is very cold-hardy. This lettuce doesn't tolerate heat well and is a spring-only crop. Thomas Jefferson grew Tennis Ball, and it was first listed in seed catalogs in 1804.

(55 Days)

Cos (Romaine)

Rouge D'Hiver

Rouge D'Hiver's heads grow to 12 inches tall with a crisp, creamy yellow-bronze center that is tender in texture and has intense flavor. An early and attractive romaine, its large leaves have a refined and bold taste; bitterness is slow to develop. Also called Little Leprechaun, Cimarron, and Red Winter, this deep red romaine is an heirloom from the eighteenth century. Plants are cold hardy and can be put in the ground when nighttime temperatures are still below freezing. Rouge D'Hiver tolerates temperatures as low as 25 degrees F or lower if it's covered at night.

(55 to 65 Days)

Ballon

Sweet, crunchy, and slightly savoyed, this French heirloom was first listed in catalogs in 1885. Ballon forms tall, classically shaped heads with large hearts that are sweeter than the outer leaves. It's both heat and cold tolerant and doesn't bolt to form a seedhead. This variety is good both for hot and cold climates.

(75 Days)

Cos (Romaine)

Ruben's Red

Crunchy, mildly sweet, juicy, and without bitterness—that's what this miniature romaine offers. Deeply savoyed, cranberry red outer leaves fade to lime green at Ruben's Red's heart. When the leaves are picked young, they add plenty of color and flavor to baby lettuce mixes. The rich leaf color becomes even deeper in cold weather. Harvest heads when they are about 7 to 8 inches tall for the best flavor. It's also called Ruben's Dwarf and Baby Red Romaine.

(55 to 60 Days)

Paris White

This heirloom romaine has more vitamins and antioxidants than any other lettuce. Paris White's light green outer leaves are juicy and sweet and the white heart retains that sweetness and crunch. It produces 8- to 10-inch-tall, upright heads that weigh up to 2 pounds. Grown in Europe for more than two centuries, Paris White was called the best romaine for gardens in 1904 by the U. S. Department of Agriculture. Don't confuse Paris White with Parris Island Cos, which is a hybrid from South Carolina.

(55 to 80 Days)

Chapter Nine

Melons

Melons originated almost five thousand years ago in the Kalahari Desert of Africa, where botanists have found their wild ancestors still growing. Watermelons are 90 percent water, and even today, they are grown in sub-Sahara Africa as a way to provide water. The watermelon also contains plenty of potassium and magnesium to prevent dehydration. Early explorers carried smaller melons as a type of water canteen.

Melons migrated north through Egypt, and during the Roman era they were cultivated and prized. In the first century, Pliny The Elder, the Roman naturalist, wrote about a plant called *melopepo* that grew on a vine but did not hang like a cucumber, but was found on the ground. He describes its fruit as spherical and yellowish and even notes that it detaches easily from the stem, all of which sounds like a cantaloupe. Melons spread eastward along the Silk Road and across Europe, flourishing in the warmer Mediterranean areas such as Spain and Portugal.

Muskmelons and watermelons were documented in 1629 in Massachusetts and were also found growing in Native American gardens. Once again, it was master gardener Thomas Jefferson who introduced many melons to the United States at his Virginian farm Monticello. But it was in Southern states such as Georgia and North Carolina that watermelons took hold as commercial crops. During the Civil War, Confederate Army soldiers boiled watermelons to make molasses for cooking. By the 1800s, most seed companies, including W. Atlee Burpee, were developing their own melon varieties by selection and selling the seeds.

Heat rules when it comes to flavorful melons: the hotter the weather, the sweeter the melon. So if you want a watermelon or cantaloupe brimming with sugar, plant in hot summer areas and in the Deep South. Or plant an heirloom melon; varieties such as Blenheim Orange or Cream of Saskatchewan deliver as much sweetness and complex flavor when grown in a New England garden as any hybrid melon from the torrid Rio Grande Valley along the Texas-Mexico border. It's their genes, honed by selecting plants with the best flavor and the most sweetness over generations, that give heirlooms the advantage.

In the Kitchen with Doreen

Melons

Knowing when to pick a melon can be tricky. Cantaloupes and muskmelons slip off their vines easily when they're ripe. Honeydews are ready to eat when their blossom ends are soft. Watermelon is the most perplexing; the best gauge is to wait until the ground spot (where it sits on the ground) is a golden yellow.

Cantaloupes and muskmelons become more flavorful and soften after being picked. Leave them at room temperature until a sweet, musky perfume is detected.

Make watermelon vinegar by scraping the rinds and mashing flesh for its juice; then strain to remove seeds and bits of flesh. Pour the mixture into crockery jugs or opaque jars and loosely cork or cap. Place in the sun for several weeks, checking periodically. The liquid will turn clear, indicating vinegar has been formed, but it's very bitter. With time, the bitterness goes away and the melon liquid develops a true vinegar taste. Seal the jars and store for use later. (This recipe came from *The American Agriculturist*, 1843.)

All whole melons can be refrigerated up to five days without loss of flavor or nutrients. Cut melons start to lose flavor immediately, even if wrapped in plastic or in sealed containers.

Watermelon salsa is the perfect topping for grilled fish like flounder or tilapia. Chop into bite-size chunks and toss with minced scallions, cilantro, and a jalapeño pepper. Squeeze lime juice over the mixture and refrigerate for 20 minutes before serving.

Melons are low in calories and sugar, have no fat, sodium, or cholesterol, and are packed with potassium, vitamin C, and magnesium. They also contain the amino acid arginine, which promotes fat burning. Fiber in melons also slows digestion, making you feel full for a long time after eating a slice or two.

Melon Salsa

Makes 3 cups

1 cup finely diced cantaloupe
   (¼ medium cantaloupe)
1 cup finely diced mango
   (1 medium mango)
1 cup finely diced papaya
   (½ medium papaya)
½ small red onion, finely chopped
½ clove garlic, minced
½ jalapeño chile, seeded and finely chopped
4 to 5 stems cilantro, leaves chopped
Juice of 1 lime
Salt, to taste
Freshly ground pepper, to taste

Combine all ingredients in a large bowl. The salsa can be kept in a tightly covered container in the refrigerator for 2 days.

Melon Granita

Makes 2 servings

1 extra-ripe cantaloupe, muskmelon,
   or Charentais melon
Mint sprigs

Cut the melon in half. Discard the seeds and scoop out the flesh, reserving the melon rind halves. Purée the flesh in a blender or food processor. Freeze the purée for 1 hour, until slushy. Fill the melon rind halves with the granita, top with the mint sprigs, and serve immediately.

Variation: For appetizer portions, cut 3 large oranges in half. Remove the pulp and set it aside for another use. Serve the melon granita in the hollow orange halves. Makes 6 servings.

Cantaloupe & Muskmelon

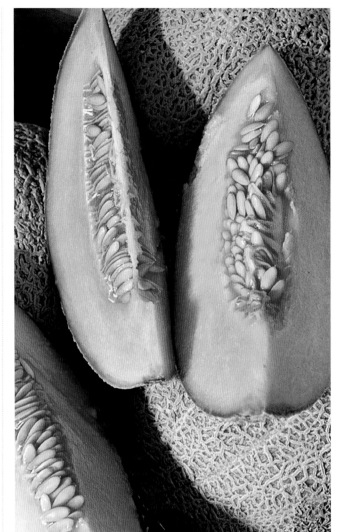

Hale's Best

Hale's Best's flesh is solid, salmon-orange in color, aromatic, and intensely sweet. Its heavily netted melons weigh up to 3 pounds. This commercial heirloom originated in Japan and has been grown in California fields since before 1923. Plants produce abundantly and are disease resistant.

(75 to 85 Days)

Blenheim Orange

Blenheim Orange's thick, succulent, red-orange flesh is highly perfumed and sweet. Melons weigh about 2 pounds each. A reliable producer, plants grow steadily through the summer, even if the weather is cool; it's an excellent choice for northern climates. This English heirloom, named for Blenheim Palace in 1891, was grown as a glasshouse or greenhouse crop for over 50 years all over the British Isles. Cover maturing melons with netting or wire screens to keep squirrels and raccoons—which are attracted by the melon's strong fragrance—away.

(90 Days)

Jenny Lind

Musky sweetness fills every bite of the white-green flesh of Jenny Lind. This small muskmelon (averaging 16 ounces) is slightly flattened with a large button on the blossom end; its skin is a dull greenish beige mottled with green. Vines are small, about 5 feet long, and prolific. Named for singer Jenny Lind, who was known as the Swedish Nightingale, this heirloom originally came from Armenia. It was first listed in seed catalogs in 1846.

(70 to 85 Days)

Watermelon

Cream of Saskatchewan

The flesh is creamy white and exceptionally sweet for a northern watermelon variety. This Russian heirloom migrated to Saskatchewan and flourished because of its genetic propensity for cool climates. The round 5- to 8-pound melons have such a thin, brittle rind that they split easily; eat them as soon as possible after picking.

(80 to 85 Days)

Moon & Stars

Moon & Stars has rinds that are thick, and its pink flesh is extra sweet with honeyed notes. Perfectly round, splashed with yellow splotches that look like heavenly bodies in a dark summer sky, Moon & Stars is a gorgeous addition to any garden. The leaves are also dotted with yellow stars. This melon requires a long, hot growing season for the best flavor. Believed to have come to the U.S. from Russia, the Amish grew Moon & Stars for generations. It's also called Cherokee Moon and Stars.

(95 to 105 Days)

Watermelon

Georgia Rattlesnake

Sweet, juicy, and huge—that easily sums up this Southern heirloom from the 1830s. Melons are almost cigar-shaped and average 35 pounds, but can weigh up to 75 pounds. Its name comes from the "rattlesnake" markings on its deep green rind. Other names are Rattlesnake, Genuine Georgia Rattlesnake, Southern Rattlesnake, and Gypsy Oblong.

(90 to 100 Days)

Kleckley Sweet

More than 160 years old, this Texas heirloom has deep red, crisp, sugary flesh and huge white seeds. The oblong, dark green melons have thin skins and weigh about 35 pounds. Kleckley Sweet grows best where summers are long and hot. W. Atlee Burpee's seed catalog introduced it in 1897. It's also called Monte Cristo.

(80 to 90 Days)

Watermelon

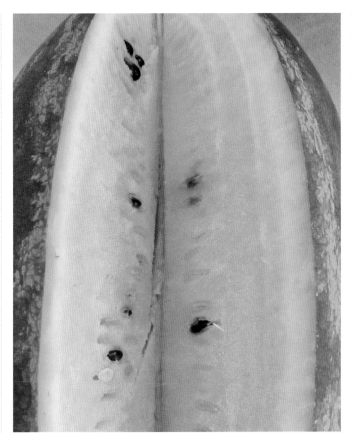

Tohono O'odham Yellow Meated

These oval green watermelons have sweet, crisp, yellow flesh. Their black seeds are eaten and used for their oil. Vines produce abundantly and fruit can weigh up to 35 pounds. Originally collected at Queenswell, Arizona, this native was introduced into Mexico by the Spanish and migrated northward to the Colorado River basin centuries ago.

(85 to 95 Days)

Sugar Baby

Intensely flavorful, this open-pollinated small watermelon has been the standard for taste since the early 1940s. Sugar Baby's personal-sized melons (1 to 2 pounds each) have vivid red flesh, small seeds, and a deep green rind. Six-foot vines usually produce four to six melons. Watch for the rind to turn almost black as a signal to harvest.

(75 to 80 Days)

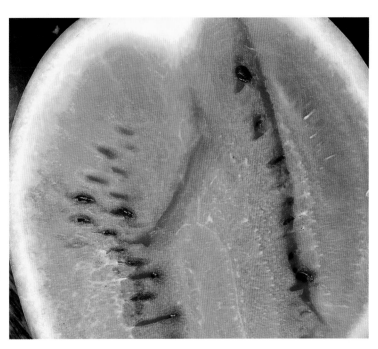

Other

Tigger

Powerfully fragrant and electrifying in appearance, this Armenian heirloom has a rich, deep melon flavor without being overly sweet. Tigger's flesh is white and quite aromatic. Its 1-pound fruits are covered with lemon yellow and fire-engine-red zigzag stripes; occasionally, a melon will be solid yellow. Vines are productive and are drought tolerant.

(85 to 90 Days)

Queen Anne's Pocket

Grown for its intense fragrance, the 3-inch melons are jaggedly striped in orange and yellow. Queen Anne's Pocket's flesh is white with a hint of honeydew and perfect for filling with icy lemon or melon granita. Persian in origin, this heirloom was introduced to England from Portugal in the late 1700s. In an era not known for personal hygiene, Victorian women carried this small, strongly perfumed melon in their pockets. You can put a bowl of them on a table to perfume the house, or grow plants near a patio or deck where the fragrant ripening melons can be enjoyed. It's also called Plum Granny.

(80 to 90 Days)

Petit Gris de Rennes

Probably the most aromatic melon ever, this 400-year-old French heirloom has deep orange flesh with an intense sweetness and a hint of muskiness. Fruits weigh 2 to 3 pounds each and have smooth gray rind with wide ribs. Petit Gris de Rennes is an early-maturing melon and well adapted to cool climates. As a Charentais type melon, harvesting can be tricky; look for the beginnings of cracks around the stem and pick if you see them. Don't wait, because wide cracks in the rind will develop, allowing bacteria to invade.

(80 to 85 Days)

Chapter Ten

Onions and Garlic

Centuries ago, wild onions and garlic grew so abundantly near Lake Michigan that Native Americans referred to that spot by the same word they used for stinky plants and skunks. That word sounded like *chicago,* and that is where the Chicago Loop is now located.

Onions and garlic are part of the same botanical family, Allium, and they share a reputation as vegetables with pungent odors, ancient beginnings, and strong opinions as to their culinary value. They were one of the earliest cultivated foods and probably among the first vegetables routinely eaten by primitive hunter-gatherers, who could easily identify them due to the onion's strong aroma. The humble onion is easy to grow and imparts wonderful flavor to cooked food, but raw, it stinks, brings tears to the eye, and bestows onion breath. Onions originated in central Asia and have been planted since about 3,000 B.C. During the Civil War, doctors used onion juice to sterilize wounds, believing that anything that burned the eyes and smelled so strong had antiseptic properties. It was believed well into the twentieth century that onion is an aphrodisiac. With that kind of reputation, legions of legislators have done their darnedest to outlaw, malign, and prosecute the onion including a law from Headland, Alabama, where it's illegal for a man to put his arms around or kiss a woman if he has eaten onions within the past four hours.

The American history of garlic is short and scant. Early settlers didn't like its taste or aroma. It took the great immigrations of the early 1900s to bring garlic and the cuisines that highlighted the assertive, pungent bulb for people to start eating it. Until about 1930, garlic was found almost exclusively in ethnic dishes in working-class neighborhoods. By 1940, America had accepted garlic, finally recognizing its value as not only a minor seasoning, but as a major ingredient in recipes. Today, Americans annually eat more than 250 million pounds of garlic, which has been shown to lower both blood pressure and cholesterol. It's also a strong antibacterial, antifungal, and antiviral herb. Raw garlic contributes the most benefits to health.

In the Kitchen with Doreen

Onions and Garlic

It's the sulfur in onions that causes your eyes to tear when you peel them. Refrigerate onions for a couple of hours before peeling to reduce the release of the offending chemicals. If you don't have time to chill the onion, peel it under running water. Cut off the onion tip last to further reduce the release of those noxious smells. To remove the onion odor from your hands when you've finished peeling, slicing, and dicing, wash them in cold water and rub a teaspoon of salt over your palms. Rinse in cold water again.

Remove strong garlic odor from your hands by wetting them in cold water, rubbing them across a stainless steel surface such as a sink or pan bottom, and then rinsing them in cold water again. This trick works for strong smelling herbs like cilantro too.

Make yummy garlic-smashed potatoes fast by boiling 2 pounds of new potatoes with their skins on and 5 cloves of peeled garlic. When the potatoes and garlic are tender, drain them; mash with a large fork. Add 2 tablespoons milk or chicken broth, fresh-ground black pepper, and ½ cup shredded sharp cheddar cheese. Mash again and serve. If you like it spicy, add a jalapeño or habanero pepper to the pot when you boil the garlic and potatoes.

To rid yourself of garlic breath, chew fresh parsley. Its chlorophyll efficiently breaks down sulfur compounds that create garlic breath. If parsley isn't available, chew some fresh mint or suck on some lemon slices.

If you chew gum while peeling onions, you won't cry. Try it!

Roasted garlic makes the ultimate garlic bread. Bake whole heads in a 400 degree F oven for 30 minutes. Then squeeze the garlic heads to release the cooked cloves. Season with a dash of sea salt and lemon juice. Spread on toasted bread and serve. Yummy!

Smashed-Onion Jam

Makes 2 cups

1½ pounds small onions, peeled
1½ cups sugar
1 cup water
2 cups white vinegar
½ cup dry white wine
2 tablespoons kosher salt
2 bay leaves
3 sprigs fresh thyme

Smash the onions using the flat side of a large knife. Combine the sugar, water, vinegar, wine, and salt in a large saucepan over low heat. Stir to dissolve the sugar. Add the onions, bay leaves, and thyme. Raise the heat to medium-high and bring to a boil. Reduce the heat to a simmer and cook, stirring occasionally, for about 1½ hours, until the onions are translucent and the liquid has been reduced to a syrup. Remove from the heat and cool before serving. Serve cold or at room temperature. The jam can be refrigerated in a tightly covered container for up to 2 weeks.

Three Onion Tart

Serves 8

Prepared pastry dough for a 9-inch pie pan
2 tablespoons olive oil
2 tablespoons butter
2 large yellow onions
8 green onions, white and green parts,
    sliced
3 garlic cloves, chopped
2 teaspoons fresh thyme leaves
1 (11 ounce) package fresh goat cheese
1 (15 ounce) can artichoke hearts, drained
Salt and freshly ground pepper
1½ cups heavy cream
4 eggs
½ teaspoon freshly ground nutmeg

Preheat the oven to 350 degrees F. Heat the olive oil and butter in a large pan over medium heat; add the onions, green onions, and garlic. Sauté until the onions caramelize, about 10 minutes. Add the thyme. Remove from the heat and allow it to cool.

Roll the pastry dough on a lightly floured surface, and position it in a 9-inch pie pan or tart pan. Prick the bottom of the crust several times with a fork. Place the pan on a baking sheet and bake for 10 minutes, or until lightly browned. Remove from the oven and let cool.

Spread the goat cheese, artichoke hearts, and caramelized onions on top of the pastry shell. Season with the salt and pepper. Whisk the cream, eggs, and nutmeg, and pour over the onion mixture. Bake 30 minutes, or until the center does not wiggle. Remove from the oven, and let cool for 5 minutes. Serve warm.

Onion

Yellow Sweet Spanish

A strong sulfur taste with plenty of sweetness makes for an onion that has been popular since the 1800s. Yellow Sweet Spanish is a major commercial crop today, but most of those grown are a hybridized version of the heirloom. Look for seeds that are open-pollinated to be sure you are getting the heirloom. Its large globes—up to 2 pounds—are the classic slicing onions, producing big, thick rings suitable for pickling and making deep-fried onion rings. The mature bulbs store well for three or four months if their thick necks have dried completely. Because it's a long-day type, don't grow this heirloom in Southern climates.

(95 to 130 Days)

Flat of Italy

This Italian variety, mentioned in 1885, is brimming with fresh sweetness. It's perfect for grilling and kebabs. A brilliant red cipollini-type gourmet onion, Flat of Italy's flattened red globes are 1 inch high and 2 to 3 inches in diameter. It should be eaten shortly after harvest for the best flavor. This red onion is the earliest to mature in the garden, making it a good choice for eating fresh. Store in mesh bags in a cool, dry location to extend their life a few months. It's an intermediate-day type, meaning it can be grown in most climates.

(70 Days)

Yellow Globe

Strong oniony flavor makes this French heirloom good for cooking; the same compounds that give the onion its intense taste also make it good for long-term storage. Coppery yellow skin covers white, firm, fine-grained flesh. It's a medium-sized, long-day variety; don't plant it in Southern climates. Yellow Globe, also called Yellow Globe Danvers, was first grown in the U.S. before 1850 around Danvers, Massachusetts.

(100 to 110 Days)

Red Torpedo

Spicy, tangy taste and purplish coloring make Red Torpedo a winner in salads. It's an intermediate-day onion that can be grown in the South and North. Bottle-shaped bulbs are 8 inches long and 3 inches in diameter, and can weigh a pound each. They can be stored briefly, but they are best eaten fresh. This heirloom from the 1800s is still widely grown for specialty markets. It's also called Italian Red Bottle and Ox Horn.

(95 to 120 Days)

Southport White Globe

White onions have a milder flavor than red or yellow ones; this heirloom from 1906 is mild, but it has a stronger sulfur taste than other whites. It's a good compromise for cooking or as a zippy topping for a freshly grilled burger. Medium-sized globes have papery white skin and are very firm; they hold that firmness in storage too. A long-day variety, Southport is best grown in northern areas. It's also called Silver Ball, White Rocco, and White Globe.

(110 to 120 Days)

Multiplier Onion

Yellow Potato Onion

Full of flavor and light on the sulfur compounds, this heirloom dates prior to 1790. Many gardeners before the 1940s planted only this variety, as it supplied everything they needed in an onion, from green onions in spring to mature bulbs for storing. Plants form clusters of 4-inch onions under ideal conditions, or 3-inch clusters during hotter summers. Yellow Potato Onion has good drought resistance and is widely adapted to different growing regions, except Florida and south Texas. The small- to medium-sized bulbs can be stored up to 12 months under good conditions. Seeds can be planted either in fall or spring sets too. Other names are Yellow Multiplier, Hill Onion, Mother Onion, and Pregnant Onion.

(130 to 250 Days)

l'itoi's

Pink-skinned and a clumping shallot type, this onion tastes like shallots with a strong flavor that doesn't linger on the tongue. Introduced by the Spanish to Mexico and the Southwest, this heirloom thrives even in drought. Easy to grow, plant onion sets in fall about 1 inch deep and a foot apart. They produce green tops and bulbs during winter in warm climates and do their growing during summer in cold-winter areas. Don't worry if the tops brown and die back during intense summer heat; they will return. Propagate by division in spring. Grow them anywhere, as these multipliers are not day-length sensitive.

(Perennial)

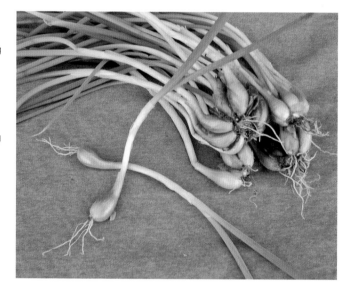

Multiplier Onions

Multiplier onions form clusters of onions up to 4 inches each in clumps. Smaller offsets can be harvested for sets to use for planting the following year. Most varieties are hardy enough to overwinter in the ground and produce again. A perennial onion in many climates, plant seeds directly in the ground during fall, rather than spring.

Softneck Garlic

Inchelium Red

A Native American heirloom discovered on the Colville Reservation in Inchelium, Washington, Inchelium Red's 3-inch bulbs have a mild, lingering flavor that sharpens with storage. Bulbs have nine to twenty-two cloves and can be grown in any climate.

Silverskin

Silverskin's classic garlic taste and mild aroma make it excellent as an all-around cooking garlic. Freshly harvested, it's perfect for braiding. Although it's an heirloom, this white-skinned bulb is what is found in most grocery stores. Each bulb averages fourteen large cloves that are easy to peel. Silverskin stores for up to a year. Recommended for all climates, especially the South and hot, dry areas. It's also called Mild French Silverskin.

(Garlic's maturity varies widely, depending on climate, latitude, and weather.)

Hardneck Garlic

Chesnok Red

The strong, hot flavor of Chesnok Red cloves makes this very aromatic heirloom a good baking and roasting garlic because its distinctive flavor is retained. Extra-large cloves (eight to twelve per bulb) are covered with purple striped skin; the bulb is covered with maroon skin. This heirloom originated in the Georgia Republic of the former Soviet Union.

German Extra Hardy

Huge cream-colored cloves with burgundy pinstripes have a strong, robust taste. There are four to six cloves per bulb, which store up to six months. Extremely cold hardy, German Extra Hardy grows best in northern climates.

Hardneck Garlic

Music Pink

Hearty taste, large size, and rich flavor make Music Pink the perfect roasting garlic. Its medium hot, true garlic flavor lingers and stands up to cooking and pickling. Pale, pink-skinned bulbs can be stored from 9 to 12 months. There are five to seven mammoth cloves per bulb. Music Pink is very cold tolerant. Another name for it is Music.

Russian Giant

Russian Giant has a strong garlic flavor and a warm, sweet aftertaste. This heirloom was brought to British Columbia by Doukhobor immigrants from Russia in the early 1900s. Its colossal bulbs look like purple mountains with a snowcap. Each has four to six gigantic tan-skinned cloves which are easy to peel. The plants look like small trees because their tops can grow up to 5 feet tall in well-fertilized ground.

Chapter Eleven

Peas

When I was growing up, peas were the first fresh vegetables out of the garden and so much tastier than the thick pea soup we cooked to a paste and flavored with a ham bone. Stone-age populations and the ensuing developing civilizations had also subsisted on similar boiled gruels of peas. In Roman times, fried peas were sold and eaten at the Roman circus and in theaters as a snack, just like popcorn is today. Hot pea soup, laced with mint to disguise its starchy taste, was peddled on the streets of Athens.

But it wasn't until the 1600s that Europeans began to eat the first sweet, tender peas of spring and found them *delicious*. Before, peas were left to dry in their pods for a storable high-protein food. When they were boiled, the peas turned into a mush that was easily consumed and could be dressed up with boiled root vegetables such as carrots and turnips. Add a meaty bone, and a hearty stew filled the air with tantalizing aromas and stomachs with a substantial meal.

There are three general types of peas grown today, and many of them are heirlooms. Shelling pea pods are split open to harvest tender, sweet green peas for fresh consumption. Any leftover can be frozen or canned for later use. Or, leave the pods and seeds to mature and dry for cooking. Snap peas, including sweet green peas, are harvested when they're young and tender. Eat them fresh, steam, freeze, or stir-fry for the best flavor. Snow peas are picked for their tender, juicy pods; the peas inside are insignificant. Snow peas are best used fresh or in stir-fry dishes.

Peas, like a few other vegetables, have changed little with the passing of time. Sweetness and vivid green color are the gauges by which an excellent fresh pea is judged. Heirlooms offer these hallmarks, surpassing most hybrids that were developed for uniformity of size and picking time. Select a pea from each category for your garden or farmers' market this year and taste all that an heirloom pea can be.

In the Kitchen with Doreen

Peas

Add a couple of washed pods to the water when you cook green peas to give them more flavor and a vibrant color.

Fresh green peas should be refrigerated after they're picked. Half of their sugar content will turn to starch within six hours if they are kept at room temperature.

Snip the tender terminal growth on pea vines (pea sprouts) early in spring for a sweet addition to salads or as a topping on sandwiches.

Snap off the stem ends of snow and sugar snap peas, and remove the string before cooking or serving raw. I do this after picking and then refrigerate the peas for snacks and salads. They'll stay crisp in the refrigerator up to five days.

Peas are high-protein vegetables, second only to beans. They are also packed with vitamins A and C, plus plenty of fiber. One serving of peas contains the amount of vitamin C in two oranges!

For a protein-packed breakfast, sauté fresh peas with diced ham and use the mixture to fill omelets.

For an extra-quick and easy recipe using fresh peas, combine 1 tablespoon of freshly squeezed lemon juice, 8 ounces of sugar snap peas (strings removed and sliced thinly on the bias), and 2 tablespoons extra-virgin olive oil. Season with salt and pepper. That's it.

To get picky kids to eat peas (and other vegetables), try offering them raw. Naked. Right there on the plate. Peas are naturally sweet, so many kids love them when they are not "dressed up." Kids also love to help, so let them shell peas with you; it's fun to eat something you helped prepare.

Spring Pea and Potato Salad

Makes 4 servings

1 pound new potatoes
1 cup fresh peas
⅓ cup mayonnaise
2 tablespoons minced fresh chives
1 teaspoon prepared mustard
2 tablespoons chopped fresh tarragon
*   or 2 teaspoons tarragon vinegar*

Steam or roast the potatoes and cool. Chop the potatoes into small chunks with skins intact. Add the potatoes and peas to a large bowl.

Combine the mayonnaise, chives, mustard, and tarragon or tarragon vinegar in a small bowl. Add the dressing to the salad and toss. Chill for at least 30 minutes before serving.

Peas and Carrots with Cream

Makes 6 servings

3 cups fresh peas
2 carrots, diced
2 teaspoons salt
1 teaspoon white pepper
1 bay leaf
¼ onion, minced
1 pint cream
1 tablespoon minced fresh dill

Place the peas in a saucepan with the carrots. Cover with water and add the salt, pepper, and bay leaf. Bring to a boil. Reduce the heat to medium-high and cook for about 10 minutes, until tender. Drain.

Meanwhile, place the onion in a large saucepan and add the cream. Bring to a simmer. Simmer until the cream is reduced by half. Remove from the heat. Place the peas and carrots in the saucepan and stir. Return to the heat and cook until the vegetables are heated. Stir in the dill and serve immediately.

Shelling

Dwarf Telephone

These late-maturing dwarf plants produce plenty of sweet pods and peas. Each broad and pointed pod contains at least nine light green peas. Dwarf Telephone was first listed in seed catalogs in 1888.

(70 to 78 Days)

Shelling

Green Arrow

All fresh peas are sweet, but some have more sugar than others. This English heirloom is about average in sugar content. Its short vines (24 to 30 inches) produce large crops of 5-inch-long slim pods filled with eight to eleven peas. Green Arrow tolerates heat and is an excellent choice for Southern gardens, even ones in Florida.

(62 to 70 Days)

Little Marvel

Sweet, dark green peas can be picked over an extended period from dwarf, bushy 16-inch-tall plants. This highly productive English variety, introduced into the U.S. in 1908, is wilt and disease resistant. Little Marvel is also called Improved American Wonder.

(58 to 64 Days)

Shelling

Lincoln

Dwarf vines of about 2 feet are loaded with small pods tightly packed with six to nine small, wrinkled, cream-colored peas. Fresh peas are slightly sweet and make an interesting addition to vegetable medleys. The dried peas of Lincoln make a delicate gourmet soup when it's seasoned with thyme and mint. Vines grow well in northern climates. Lincoln was called Homesteader before 1908.

(65 to 70 Days)

Sugar Snap

A Class III heirloom cross between an ancient Chinese snow pea and a shelling pea, Sugar Snap is the first pea to have rounded, sweet pods and plump peas, both a delight to eat raw. Created by University of Idaho plant breeders, Sugar Snap has spawned numerous Sugar Snap hybrid varieties. Many believe this original has more sweetness and flavor than any of the subsequent offspring. Vines grow up to 6 feet tall, are productive, and can tolerate light frosts.

(60 Days)

Golden Snow

This extra-sweet, lemon yellow, edible-podded Native American heirloom can also be grown as a soup bean. Mature, dried peas are tan with purple flecks. Golden Snow vines grow 6 feet tall with stunning two-toned purple flowers. Pick pods when they're small for the best flavor. The yellow pods are a tasty and gorgeous addition to Red Velvet lettuce in salads. The plants are heavy producers and tolerate heat and drought. It's also called Golden Sweet.

(60 to 70 Days)

Chapter Twelve

Peppers

Five hundred years ago, most of the world had never eaten a pepper, in any form. So although it's a new vegetable in terms of world distribution, peppers, native to tropical America, have been cultivated since 7,000 B.C. The fiery peppers migrated around the world, changing in size, form, and heat intensity. Columbus took seeds and fruits of various peppers he encountered in the New World back to Spain with him and within one hundred years, peppers became part of many of the world's best cuisines. What would Indian curry be without peppers? Or pepperoni without the hint of heat, or Hungarian stews without smoky paprika, or Indonesian sambals without their fire? (This is what's called a rhetorical question.)

And it's not just food. Native Americans burned piles of chile peppers when they fought the invading English; the fumes kept the soldiers at bay. Today, peppers are often used as tests of manhood and intestinal fortitude at many chili- and hot pepper-eating contests.

Central American tribes selected peppers without the capsicum oils that give peppers their signature heat or burn and called them pimentos or bells, after their chunky, lobed shape. These, too, migrated northward and across oceans to become part of cuisines everywhere. Most of the peppers sold in this country are bells, not the more than 3,000 hot pepper varieties available worldwide. These peppers, known for their pungency (heat), vary in intensity. That's why in 1912, Wilbur Scoville devised a scale in order to classify various peppers by their capsicum content and resulting heat units. The exponential scale runs from zero for ripe bell peppers to 350,000 units in a habanero. Pure capsicum is 16 million units; pepper spray is formulated at about 1 million units. In the Ozarks and Deep South, legend has it that in order for peppers to be hot, you have to be very angry when you plant them. (It's also said that the best peppers are planted by lunatics.) Well, I don't know about that, but I do know you'll love the flavors of these heirloom pepper varieties.

In the Kitchen with Doreen

Peppers

Let sweet peppers mature to a red color for the most vitamin C; a red pepper contains six times more vitamin C than an orange.

The heat in a hot pepper, which is the oil capsaicin, is concentrated in the seeds and membranes of a pepper. There is 100 times more of it than is in the pepper walls.

Use gloves when peeling, cutting, or cleaning hot peppers to avoid contact with the capsaicin oil. If it does get on your fingers, immediately wipe the site with white vinegar to neutralize the burn. Don't touch your eyes!

If a pepper burns your mouth, drink milk or eat a slice of cheese for relief. Beer and other alcoholic beverages not only don't stop the burn, they make it worse.

To skin peppers—especially hotter ones like the Anaheim, used for stuffing—place them under the broiler and roast until skin turns slightly black. Remove them from the oven and place in a sealed paper bag for 10 minutes to steam. Skins will slip off easily. Roasting also intensifies the flavor.

Air dry hot peppers for use in winter. Their flavor becomes more complex. Choose varieties with thin walls, like jalapeño and habanero. Tie the pepper stems to a string and hang long chains of them in a dark, dry, warm area. When they are fully dry, you can hang the ristra, as it's called, in your kitchen for easy access and a decorative note.

Soak dried peppers in hot water for 15 minutes, or until soft, before using them.

Pico de gallo is a classic relish that is simple to make. Dice a couple of firm tomatoes, two seeded jalapeños, and green onion tops. Add minced cilantro, a crushed clove of garlic, and sprinkle with lemon juice. Serve pico de gallo as a topping for tacos, enchiladas, or as a dip with corn chips. If you dare, substitute habaneros or chile tepins for the jalapeños!

Hot Blueberry Salsa

Makes 3 cups

2 cups coarsely chopped blueberries
1 cup whole blueberries
¼ cup freshly squeezed lemon juice
3 tablespoons chopped fresh cilantro
2 jalapeño chiles, seeded and minced
⅓ cup diced red bell pepper
½ teaspoon kosher salt

In a large bowl, toss together all the ingredients. Serve immediately or cover and chill for up to 8 hours.

Chiles con Queso

Makes 6 to 8 servings

½ pound feta and garlic cheese, crumbled
½ pound Monterey Jack and green chile cheese, grated
½ pound longhorn cheese, grated
½ pound Mexican cheese, grated
2 jalapeño chiles, sliced into rings
1 Anaheim chile, roasted and cut into rings
6 tablespoons bottled picante sauce, plus additional for serving
Tortilla chips

Spray a microwavable casserole dish with nonstick cooking spray. Sprinkle the cheeses in the dish in an even layer. Sprinkle the jalapeño and Anaheim chiles on top of the cheese. Top with the picante sauce. Microwave on high until bubbly. Serve with the tortilla chips and additional picante sauce.

Oven Roasted Peppers, Zucchini, Fennel, and Onion

Serves 6

2 bell peppers (a mix of colors is more fun), seeded and sliced in 2-inch-wide strips
2 medium zucchinis, trimmed and sliced diagonally
1 fennel bulb, trimmed and cut into small wedges
1 small red onion, peeled and sliced into ¼-inch-thick rounds
2 tablespoons olive oil
3 garlic cloves, minced
1 teaspoon kosher salt
½ teaspoon freshly ground pepper
4 springs fresh thyme

Preheat the oven to 375 degrees F. Place the vegetables (in groups) onto a baking sheet. Drizzle the olive oil on top, add the garlic, and toss gently to lightly coat the groups of vegetables with the oil. Using another baking sheet, spread the vegetables into one layer on the two pans; each piece should be separated instead of being crowded. Sprinkle with the salt and pepper, and place the thyme sprigs on top. Roast 15 minutes; turn the veggies over to roast on their other side for another 5 to 10 minutes. Serve hot or at room temperature.

Sweet

Merrimack Wonder

These blocky, four-lobed bell peppers have thick walls and a mildly sweet flavor. Merrimack Wonder is good for cold climates with short seasons; its flowers will set fruits even in chilly weather. It was a commercial and garden favorite before 1940.

(60 Days)

Bull Nose

When red and fully ripe, this four-lobed bell-type pepper has a crisp, sweet flavor. Its ribs have a bit of spice, adding to the complexity of each tasty bite. Plants are stocky and productive. Bull Nose originated in India in the seventeenth century, was grown by Thomas Jefferson, and was listed in catalogs by 1863.

(55 to 80 Days)

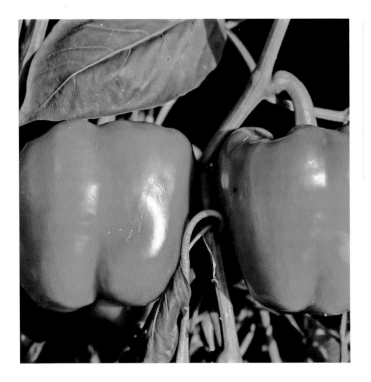

California Wonder

This large-sized stuffing pepper has extremely thick, mild, sweet flesh. California Wonder's shape is distinctly lobed, upright, shapely, and glossy dark green. Peppers mature to red, but this commercial favorite is mostly sold as a green pepper. California Wonder was introduced to California growers in 1928.

(65 to 75 Days)

Red Cherry

More than 100 years old, this tiny, chocolate-drop-shaped pepper is extra sweet and great for fresh eating and pickling. Bushy plants bear heavy crops of 1- to 1½-inch peppers. It's also called Red Cherry.

(70 Days)

Klari Baby Cheese

A sweet and crunchy treat right off the bush, this cheese-type pepper has thick walls, is petite, and is creamy white when ripe. (At the pure white stage, they have little flavor.) Try stuffing these sweeties with ground turkey and minced garlic chives. Bake 20 minutes, sprinkle with Hungarian paprika, and serve. This heirloom came from Hungary.

(65 Days)

Nardello

Long, tapered red peppers are packed with crisp sweetness; they stay fresh for days when refrigerated, even if they've been cut. At the green stage, peppers have a touch of heat. Plants are tall and should be staked or caged, as they bow under the weight of large crops of big peppers. An excellent Italian-style frying pepper, it makes superior pasta sauces. Also called Jimmy Nardello's.

(80 to 90 Days)

Hot

Rocotillo

From Peru, this ancient pepper is moderately hot (2,500 Scoville units), crunchy, and attractive. It's not unusual to have green, yellow, orange, and red peppers on plants all at once. They are hottest at the orange stage. This pepper is also called Balloon, Bishop's Hat, Fire in a Bonnet, and Peter Pepper.

(90 to 100 Days)

Fish

Colorful, crunchy and a bit hot (a Scoville reading of about 5,000 units), this heirloom was first used in oyster and crab houses around the Chesapeake Bay. Foliage is an attractive variegated green-and-white on sprawling 2-foot-tall bushes. Slightly curled 2- to 3-inch fruits ripen from cream with green stripes to orange with brown stripes and then to all red. Plants can be grown in containers as an ornamental with the peppers as an edible bonus.

(80 Days)

Chiletepine

This blazing hot pepper (up to 200,000 Scoville units) grows wild in southwestern deserts. Cowboys along the Rio Grande river used to pick them wild to flavor pots of beans and stew. They carried the peppers with them and seeds took root along trails to Ft. Worth and Kansas City when they drove cattle to market. Plants freeze back in the winter, but sprout again in USDA hardiness Zones 7 to 10. Other names are Pequin, Chile Tepin, and Bird Pepper.

(80 to 120 Days)

Anaheim

Milder than other chilies, about 500 to 2,000 Scoville units, Anaheim still has a kick. Its flavor is complex, with a touch of sugar, plenty of earthy pepper, and smoky notes, especially when roasted before eating. Peppers grow 6 to 8 inches long and are the pepper of choice for making chile rellenos. It was named by Emilio Ortego, of the canned pepper dynasty, in 1900 after the area of California where the chile pepper was discovered. It's also known as California Chile, Magdalena, and, when dried, as Chile Seco Del Norte.

(70 to 80 Days)

Jalapeño

For a hot pepper, Jalapeños are mild, with only 3,000 to 5,000 Scoville units. It has enough kick to make it the workhorse chile of Southwestern cuisines, but not enough to scorch mouths. Saturated, rich flavor can be enjoyed because the pepper's heat doesn't burn the taste buds. Pick dusky, dark green peppers with small cracks around the stem for the best flavor.

(70 to 80 Days)

Habanero

Originating on the Yucatan Peninsula, this heirloom is not only one of the hottest peppers (350,000 Scoville units) available, but it has a complex taste beyond all the heat. A strong floral aroma introduces citrus tones when you bite into the pepper. Pick peppers that are a rich orange for the most flavor.

(90 to 100 Days)

Chapter Thirteen

Potatoes

Of all the foods discovered by explorers, the potato has fed more people than any staple in the world except corn. This easily grown plant provides more nutritious food faster on less land than any other food crop, and in almost any climate. Though potatoes were first cultivated in the Lake Titicaca basin of southern Peru and Bolivia about five thousand years ago, many scientists believe potatoes may have grown wild in the steep mountains of that region as early as 700 B.C.

Those first wild potatoes had blue or purple skin full of anthocyanins, powerful antioxidant pigments. The first potatoes grew in crevices and rocky outcroppings where the soil was very shallow. Developing tubers had only a scant layer of dirt to cover them, so purple and blue pigments evolved as a natural sunshade to high levels of ultraviolet light at high altitudes. As the potato migrated to lower, more temperate, areas, its purple skin and flesh gradually evolved into brown, red, cream, and almost white colors.

Potatoes were introduced to the Americas in the 1620s when the British governor of the Bahamas sent a box of them to the governor of Virginia. However, potatoes did not become widely accepted until they received Thomas Jefferson's seal of approval. In the 1920s, the trend towards fried potatoes and French fries started, and by 1945, it was easier to find a fried potato or French fries on menus and dinner tables than boiled potatoes, the mainstay of diets around the world. Today, the average American eats about 115 pounds of potatoes a year, mostly in the form of French fries and potato chips. With a nation begging for crispy French fries, it was inevitable that an entrepreneur like Ray Kroc, founder of McDonald's, would find the perfect French fry potato. He contracted with an Idaho food processor who discovered that the Russet Burbank heirloom was the perfect potato for fries. He patented a process to turn the Russet potato (which resembles a smooth, blocky brick and is easy to peel) into the perfect French fry. The rest is history.

In the Kitchen with Doreen

Potatoes

Do not store potatoes in the refrigerator. Refrigeration converts the starch in potatoes to a form of sugar, which will cause a potato to darken when it's cooked. Store tubers in a damp, dark, and cool area in boxes or large wood bins where air circulates freely. Basements with dirt floors or those with concrete floors with a layer of moist peat moss are ideal.

Microwave blue- and red-fleshed potatoes to retain their color, or steam potatoes just to the point of tenderness. Baking, boiling, and stewing will fade colors slightly.

Blue-fleshed potatoes have more vitamins and antioxidants than any other potato. In fact, they have as much antioxidant power as Brussels sprouts, kale, and spinach combined.

If you add a squeeze of fresh lemon juice to slices when frying them, potatoes will caramelize and be crisper.

A flavorful, fast way to serve potatoes is to cut them into chunks, drizzle with olive oil, and roast in a 375 degree F oven for 40 minutes or until the chunks turn brown. Roasting unleashes complex flavors and crispness, plus it's much healthier than fried potatoes. Leave skins on, as many of the potato's nutrients are in them.

Discard green potatoes and cut away any green spots from otherwise perfect tubers. Solanine, which colors the potato green, is a toxic compound created when a developing potato is exposed to sunlight.

Place just-peeled potatoes in cold water until you're ready to cook them; they discolor otherwise.

When boiling potatoes for salad, add a teaspoon or two of vinegar to the water. Vinegar makes the potatoes form a thin crust that helps them to hold their shape.

Make a classic potato soup the easy way in your crockpot. Cube 8 large potatoes, and combine with chopped onion, 1 tablespoon butter, 2 chicken bouillon cubes, 3 cups each water and milk, and chopped fresh parsley leaves. Cook on low for 8 hours.

Baby Potato and Watercress Salad

Makes 8 servings

4 pounds new potatoes
1 tablespoon plus ½ teaspoon kosher salt
5 eggs
1 cup mayonnaise
1 tablespoon Dijon mustard
1 cup plain yogurt
2 shallots, coarsely chopped
1 clove garlic, coarsely chopped
2 tablespoons freshly squeezed lemon juice
¼ teaspoon freshly ground pepper
1 cup watercress sprigs
¼ cup finely chopped fresh chives

Place the potatoes in a large pot. Add 1 tablespoon of the salt and enough water to cover by 2 inches. Bring to a boil. Simmer until fork-tender, about 20 minutes; drain.

Place the eggs in a saucepan and add enough water to cover. Bring to a boil and cook for 8 minutes. Drain and transfer to a bowl of ice water. When cooled, peel and chop the eggs.

In a food processor or blender, process the mayonnaise, mustard, yogurt, shallots, garlic, lemon juice, pepper, and remaining ½ teaspoon salt until smooth.

Halve the potatoes and place in a serving bowl. Add the dressing and combine. Add the eggs, watercress, and chives and toss. Cover and chill for at least 3 hours before serving.

Potato Gratin with Mustard and Cheddar Cheese

Makes 12 servings

1 tablespoon dried thyme
2 teaspoons salt
1 teaspoon freshly ground pepper
1 pound white sharp Cheddar cheese, grated
¼ cup all-purpose flour
5 pounds russet potatoes, peeled and thinly sliced
4 cups low-salt chicken broth
1 cup heavy whipping cream
6 tablespoons Dijon mustard

Position the rack in the center of the oven and preheat the oven to 400 degrees F. Butter a 15 x 10-inch (2-quart) glass baking dish.

Mix the thyme, salt, and pepper in a small bowl. Combine the cheese and flour in a large bowl, tossing to coat the cheese. Arrange one-third of the potatoes in the bottom of the prepared baking dish. Sprinkle with one-third of the thyme mixture, then one-third of the cheese mixture. Repeat layering the potatoes, thyme mixture, and cheese mixture two more times. Whisk together the broth, cream, and mustard in a medium bowl. Pour the broth mixture over the potatoes.

Bake the potatoes for 30 minutes. Continue baking until the potatoes are tender and the top is golden brown, about 1 hour longer. Let stand for 15 minutes before serving.

Early Maturing

Irish Cobbler

Irish Cobbler has a pronounced potato flavor with a nutty aroma in the skin when it's cooked. This offspring of Early Rose, dating to 1885, is also an exquisite boiling potato. It has smooth light brown skin and white flesh. Tubers bruise easily and have a short storage life, like most early potatoes.

(75 to 90 Days)

Caribe

The smooth purplish red skin and creamy white flesh of Caribe are a treat to the eyes and palate. Its fresh, earthy *zing* and high sugar content make Caribe great for mashing and frying. Grown in the late 1800s in New England for export to the Caribbean, Caribe was a profitable export crop because of its uniformly sized tubers and heavy yields.

(60 to 75 Days)

Early Rose

Early Rose has red skin with a creamy flesh that often has a pale pink halo. Packed with fresh potato flavor, it's excellent for baking and boiling. This low-starch potato has been popular since 1861. The parent of Luther Burbank's Russet (the McDonald's French fry potato) Early Rose is easy to grow in any climate or soil type. Antwerp, Boston Market, and Chicago Market are some of the other names for Early Rose.

(60 to 75 Days)

All Red

Another colorful tuber, with red skin and pale pink flesh, All Red makes creamy, sublime scalloped potatoes. It's an ideal boiling potato because of its low starch content, and it holds its shape. Plants produce abundantly and tubers store up to 8 months. Also called Cranberry Red, this heirloom grows well even during drought.

(70 to 90 Days)

Lady Finger

Long, slim tubers (5 to 6 inches long and 1 inch in diameter) grow connected to one another like ginger root. Lady Finger's flesh is yellow and sweet. Brought to the U.S. by German immigrants, Lady Finger is still grown extensively in Texas, where many Germans settled and farmed.

(80 to 90 Days)

All Blue

Nutty and moist, these beauties are excellent in salads and when roasted. All Blue, also known as Purple Marker, is an all-around potato with medium starch content. The deep blue-purple skin and flesh of these potatoes indicate they are probably the most direct descendent of wild potatoes found in the Peruvian mountains.

(70 to 90 Days)

Late Maturing

Russian Banana Fingerling

Its rich buttery flavor makes Russian Banana Fingerling perfect for skins-on mashed potatoes, roasting, and a potato salad that sets the standard with its mouth-feel and subtle nutty flavor. A favorite of gourmet chefs, these small banana-shaped tubers of Russian origin have light yellow or buff skin and yellow, waxy flesh. They're scab-resistant and store well in a cool, dark place for 3 months or more.

(105 to 135 Days)

German Butterball

Its pronounced buttery flavor makes this 150-year-old potato variety a favorite of gardeners and farmers, even today. German Butterball is an all-purpose potato with medium starch content. The small- to medium-sized oblong tubers have delicate yellow skin and deep golden flesh. German Butterball stores up to 8 months and is disease resistant and high yielding.

(95 to 120 Days)

Bintje

Perfect for making gnocchi, the Italian potato pasta, Bintje's high starch content and firm texture are sought by cooks for their sauce-holding characteristics. These heirlooms came from the Netherlands in 1911 and have gold skin and yellow flesh. Plants tolerate drought and yield big crops. Bintje is the most widely planted yellow-fleshed potato in the world.

(100 to 120 Days)

Russet Burbank

King of the French fry and chips, this long, large potato is found in every store and labeled as a baking potato. Whether baked or deep fried, Russet Burbank crisps exquisitely on the outside because of its high sugar content. The white flesh stays fluffy and is packed with a commanding, earthy taste. Horticulturist Luther Burbank selected the potato in 1872 from an Early Rose mutant. The original tubers had smooth skins, but in 1914 Lou Sweet, a Colorado farmer, found a sport (mutation) in his fields that had heavily russeted skin. Though it was uglier, this new variety of Russet Burbank was resistant to blights, and spread across North America as the commercial potato of choice.

(120 to 150 Days)

Chapter Fourteen

Radishes

Esteemed by the Greek god Apollo, cultivated by ancient Egyptian pyramid builders, and eaten for breakfast by our Colonial fathers, the radish has been around for more than 5,000 years. They were prescribed by physicians to prevent scurvy, used by herbalists to ward off women's chatter (*what?*), and salted or pickled to accompany food and drink throughout recorded time. For thousands of years, radishes have been seen as an appetite stimulant. Ben Johnson, a contemporary of Shakespeare, suggested they be eaten before tasting wine to clear the palate.

Some linguists believe that the word "radish" comes from the Latin word *radix*, meaning root. Others insist that quick-growing radishes get their name from the Greek word meaning fast appearing.

As early as 1750, Dutch-American farmers grew radishes for their breakfast. The traditional menu consisted of tea, bread and butter, and radishes. By the end of the century, at least ten radish varieties were grown. Both spring and winter radishes were planted; the first for immediate consumption and the larger winter ones for storage.

There's much more in the radish world than the mild red and white radishes found on relish plates and in salads. Although a French Breakfast radish can perk up potato salad, also consider the zesty, rose-fleshed, white-skinned Chinese Watermelon radish, or crunchy mustard-infused radish pods. These have bold, sharp flavor! Some radishes weigh up to *5 pounds* while others offer a color explosion. Still others infuse cooked dishes with subtle flavors that are the hallmark of some ethnic foods.

The radish is still so prized that there is a Night of the Radish, or *La Noche de los Rabanos*, every December 23 in Oaxaca, Mexico. Local farmers grow giant white winter radishes that are carved into sculptures worthy of a museum. Radish bullfighters, radish Nativity scenes, and more line the village square while merrymakers dance and eat—radish tamales, radish empanadas, and radish pickles, of course—until midnight when the champion radish sculpture is awarded the grand prize. Sculpting a radish may not be your passion, but sampling a few heirlooms certainly can liven up your dinner table.

In the Kitchen with Doreen

Radishes

Remove radish tops for better storage. Those with tops last only a day or two in the refrigerator. Topless ones stay fresh up to a week.

One serving of radishes (7 small or 1 large) has only 15 calories and contributes 30 percent of the recommended daily value of vitamin C. They are low in fat and sodium too.

Most of the "heat" in radishes is in the skin. If you wish to peel any of them, use a vegetable peeler or paring knife, then slice or grate them.

Radishes make great pickles that can be prepared overnight. Start with 2 cups of sliced or chunked firm radishes. Put them in a mixing bowl and sprinkle 1 teaspoon of salt over them. Cover and chill for 30 minutes. Drain any liquid and rinse the radishes to remove the salt. Pat dry with paper towels and return them to the bowl. Add 2 tablespoons rice wine vinegar, a dash or two of ground black pepper, and a couple drops of sesame seed oil. Refrigerate at least 8 hours.

Add *zip* to salads with radish greens. Pick the leaves of immature ones, wash, and include with a blend of other salad greens. Radish greens can be used in stir-fries too. Radish greens aren't as spicy as the radish.

Thick slices of radishes make delicious appetizers when topped with sour cream dip or flavored cream cheese. Dairy products moderate the bite and accentuate the nuanced flavors of radishes.

Any large radish can be roasted with other root vegetables such as turnips and sweet potatoes for a tasty winter vegetable medley. Cut all vegetables into bite-sized chunks, drizzle with olive oil, and season with sea salt. Roast until crispy. The sweetness of the sweet potatoes tempers the radishes.

If radishes are too hot for your taste, soak them overnight in the refrigerator in cold water. Cut thin slices of the red skin almost to the root end before soaking to make radish roses for salads too.

Substitute Round Black radishes for horseradish. Its winter roots are fiery and pungent. Simply grate them and use as you would horseradish. Also, add chunks of Round Black radishes to sauerkraut or kimchee for another dimension of flavor.

Radish Salad with Blue Cheese

Makes 4 servings

¼ cup light mayonnaise
¼ cup reduced-fat sour cream
1 tablespoon red wine vinegar
1 tablespoon minced shallot
¼ teaspoon Worcestershire sauce
⅛ teaspoon freshly ground pepper
¼ cup cold water
¾ cup crumbled blue cheese (about 3 ounces), divided
2 carrots, peeled
15 medium red radishes (about 6 ounces), thinly sliced
1 head iceberg lettuce, torn into bite-sized pieces
Kosher salt

In a large bowl, whisk together the mayonnaise, sour cream, vinegar, shallot, Worcestershire sauce, pepper, and water. Stir in ½ cup of the blue cheese, breaking up any large pieces.

With a vegetable peeler, peel the carrots into long, thin ribbons. Add the carrots, radishes, and lettuce to the bowl with the dressing. Toss to combine. Season lightly with salt. Divide among 4 bowls and sprinkle with the remaining ¼ cup blue cheese. Serve immediately.

Roasted Radishes

Makes 4 servings

2 cups quartered radishes
1 tablespoon sesame oil
2 teaspoons soy sauce
Sesame seeds

Preheat the oven to 425 degrees F.

Combine the radishes, sesame oil, and soy sauce in a medium bowl. Spread in a single layer on a baking sheet. Roast for 15 minutes, until the radish edges begin to brown. Sprinkle with the sesame seeds and serve immediately.

Pasta with Radishes and Pine Nuts

Makes 6 servings

3 tablespoons extra-virgin olive oil
1 onion, chopped
25-30 radishes, trimmed, sliced thinly
1 garlic clove, minced
½ cup pine nuts, toasted
Salt
Freshly ground pepper
12 ounces penne pasta, cooked according to package directions, drained, 2 tablespoons of cooking water reserved
⅓ cup grated Parmesan cheese, plus additional for serving
½ cup chopped fresh flat-leaf parsley

Heat the olive oil in a large pan over medium-high heat. Add the onion and sauté until the onion is translucent, about 5 minutes. Add the radishes and cook about 2 minutes longer. Add the garlic and pine nuts and cook about 1-2 minutes. Remove the pan from the heat, and season with the salt and pepper. Combine the pasta, the reserved cooking water, and the radish mixture in a serving bowl, add the Parmesan cheese and parsley, and toss lightly. Serve with extra Parmesan cheese, if desired.

Podding

Rat's Tail

Distinct mustard and pepper notes with plenty of juiciness describe the first bites you'll taste of a Rat's Tail pod. Found by explorers in 1860 on the island of Java, this unusual radish's aerial growth is marked by many tall stalks. They produce multiple flowers that mature into pods. (There is no edible root.) Pick pods when they're young; the older ones are fibrous. Raw, they are crunchy additions to salads, but they can also be pickled, and they add zest to stir-fries.

(45 to 50 Days)

Munchen Bier

The pods are peppery with a trace of mild mustard flavor. The root flavor is mild yet pungent. This old European variety was often sliced thin, salted, and served with dark beer in taverns in Munich, Germany, for over 100 years. As it grows, it first produces aerial stalks with pods that can be eaten, and then a large, white tapered root develops.

(65 to 70 Days)

Early Scarlet Globe

This refreshing, extra-early radish doesn't have the hot notes of later radishes. Their uniformly round globes have red skins and crisp white flesh. Sow seeds every two weeks for a continuous harvest, from early spring until June. Henry Field's Seed Company listed Early Scarlet in their 1927 catalog and said they were the perfect market radish with exceptionally fine flavor. It's still the radish most often found in the produce section of grocery stores today.

(22 Days)

Sparkler

Juicy and sweet, the color of this round radish starts as scarlet at the top and fades gradually to white at its tip. Its flesh is white and crisp. It's *perfect* for eating out of hand, plus the greens are edible too.

(25 Days)

Spring

French Breakfast

Infused with a mild peppery flavor, these crisp, oblong, blunt-nosed
2-inch radishes have scarlet skin that fades to white at the tip.
Introduced before the 1800s, this heirloom was a favorite among
French market gardeners. American seed catalogs listed French
Breakfast beginning in the middle of the 1800s.

(20 to 30 Days)

White Icicle

If you like your spring radishes on the hot side, this one will be a favorite. Hot pepper and mustard notes fill every bite. This 5-inch-long white, carrot-shaped radish will deliver the heat even when it's picked just 20 days after seeding. They do get woody once hot weather sets in, so for an autumn harvest begin planting White Icicle radish seeds again once the temperatures cool. It was first listed in seed catalogs in 1896.

(20 to 30 Days)

German Giant

Mild and piquant, these 1-ounce, round red radishes with white flesh are always crisp. German Giant, which is very large for a spring radish, can be harvested from golf ball size up to *5 pounds*. They never get hot or woody, even if they're grown to larger sizes. This heirloom is very popular with the Amish and originally came from Germany.

(28 Days)

Winter

Round Black Spanish

Diffused with pungent crispness, these large turnip-shaped globes grow up to 3 inches in diameter with tall tops. Its skin is tar black while its flesh is white. As they are generally used for winter storage, sow this radish variety in July or August and lay them in moist sand in a dark, cool space after harvest. Round Black Spanish dates to 1824 and was distributed by the Shakers through their vast seed-saving network. They valued it for storage because they could have a vegetable to serve for breakfast and in stews during winter.

(60 to 80 Days)

Watermelon

Milder than most radishes and with a touch of sweetness, this winter radish is a treat for the eyes. It also goes by the name Shinrimei—which means "beauty in the heart" in Chinese—to reflect the beautiful red flesh and white skin. Use it in salads, or shred it to use in soups, hot pasta, or over grilled fish. Sprinkle sliced Watermelon radishes with black sesame seeds for a gorgeous tasty treat. Of Chinese origin, the 4-inch ball-shaped radishes can be harvested anytime after 50 days. The radish grows best in cool weather, making it suitable for fall or early spring crops. If planted during summer heat, the plants will flower and fail to form radishes. This heirloom variety of daikon radishes is also called Roseheart and China Rose. It was introduced to this country about 1850.

(50 to 60 Days)

Chapter Fifteen

Squash and Pumpkins

For their first Thanksgiving feast, the Pilgrims invited local Narragansett Indians to share a bounty of food that wouldn't have been possible without their neighbors' help. The previous winter, these early settlers turned up their noses at long-storing foods such as squash, pumpkin, dent corn, and pemmican (a dried paste of ground berries and game meat). Consequently, the Pilgrims went hungry until they were forced to consume the gifts from their Native American neighbors. When summer came, the colonists planted seeds given to them, harvested large crops, and tried to recreate foods similar to the ones they ate in their native England.

That first Thanksgiving dinner really *did* include pumpkin pie. Pilgrim cooks hollowed out small pumpkins and filled them with sliced apples, sugar, spices, and milk. After placing the stem cap back on the pumpkin, it was buried in hot ashes of a cooking fire and baked until tender. After that first experience, squash and pumpkins quickly became diet staples.

Throughout the centuries, squash and pumpkins have been referred to as "squash" if they were smaller, and as "pumpkin" if larger; many called both as squash. Squash are one of the oldest known crops of the New World, more than 10,000 years by some estimates. Since squash are gourds, they likely served as containers or utensils because of their hard shells. The seeds and flesh later became an important part of the pre-Columbian diet in South and North America. Explorers like DeSoto and Coronado saw "melons" (probably squash) in the Americas and wrote about them. Native Americans in what is now the northeastern United States grew pumpkins, yellow crooknecks, and patty pan squash. Southern tribes raised winter crooknecks, cushaws, and green-and-white striped squash. All tribes roasted or boiled their squash and preserved the flesh in syrup (conserve). They also ate young shoots, leaves, and flowers from the plants and roasted the seeds. When you select an heirloom pumpkin like Long Island Cheese or the prolific White Patty Pan summer squash, you're perpetuating American history that dates thousands of years, not to mention enjoying flavors you won't get at a grocery store.

In the Kitchen with Doreen

Squash and Pumpkins

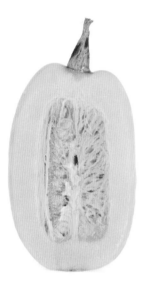

Zucchini or Yellow Crookneck squash make quick appetizers or vegetable courses. Heat an oven to 450 degrees F and cut the squash into wedges. Brush the wedges with olive oil and roll in chopped fresh oregano. Bake 10 to 12 minutes. Sprinkle grated Parmesan or Asiago cheese on top, and bake another 2 to 3 minutes or until the cheese melts. You can also grill them!

Pumpkin seeds are a nutritious snack. Subtly sweet and nutty with a chewy texture, the roasted seeds are one of the most nutritious and flavorful seeds around. Clean and gently roast with a little light oil, sprinkled with salt, or eat them raw.

Winter squash and pumpkin develop more beta-carotene during storage than if they're eaten at harvest.

Use Blue Hubbard winter squash and pleated Rouge Vif d'Etampes pumpkins for fall decorations along with mum plants, gourds, and corn shocks. Then use them for the Thanksgiving meal. Both can be baked whole and their soft flesh scooped out for pies, soups, and breads.

The blossoms from both summer and winter squash are edible. Pick them when buds are closed. They're a lovely garnish and can be stuffed with ricotta cheese and cooked mushrooms or deep-fried.

Sliced or grated raw summer squash makes a tasty addition to green salads.

Grated summer squash is also a handy substitute for carrots in carrot cake. Spices in the cake overpower the vegetable's flavor, and you cannot taste any difference.

For a nutritious dinner your kids will love, scoop out the seeds and membrane of a medium-sized pumpkin. Preheat the oven to 350 degrees F. Add 1 pound ground turkey, 2 cups cooked brown rice, one can cream of chicken soup, and diced bell peppers and onions. Put the "lid" on the filled pumpkin and bake for 1½ hours. Include the soft pumpkin flesh when you spoon out portions.

Summer Squash Tart with Olives

Makes 4 servings

3 tablespoons coarsely chopped fresh flat-leaf parsley
2 tablespoons coarsely chopped fresh oregano, plus sprigs for garnish
1 tablespoon coarsely chopped fresh thyme
1 clove garlic, minced
¼ cup extra-virgin olive oil, divided
Kosher salt
Freshly ground pepper
2 small zucchini, cut into ⅛-inch-thick rounds
2 small yellow summer squash, cut into ⅛-inch-thick rounds
6 sheets phyllo dough (each 17 x 12 inches), thawed if frozen
3 tablespoons unsalted butter, melted
½ cup pitted kalamata olives

Preheat the oven to 375 degrees F. Brush a rimmed baking sheet with butter.

In a small bowl, stir together the parsley, oregano, thyme, garlic, and 3 tablespoons of the oil; season with salt and pepper. Toss the zucchini and squash with the remaining 1 tablespoon oil in a separate bowl; season with salt and pepper.

Unfold the dough and cover each sheet with a clean, slightly damp kitchen towel. Press 1 sheet of dough into the prepared baking sheet. Lightly brush the dough with butter. Repeat, layering the remaining 5 sheets dough and brushing each with butter.

Spread the herb mixture over the dough. Spread the zucchini and squash on top; top with the olives. Bake until the edges are browned, 25 to 30 minutes. Let cool slightly. Cut into 6 pieces and garnish with the oregano sprigs. Leftover pieces can be refrigerated in a tightly covered container for up to 1 day.

Yellow Squash with Hazelnuts and Pecorino

Makes 4 servings

1 tablespoon extra-virgin olive oil
3 medium yellow squash, cut into 3-inch wedges
½ cup raw blanched hazelnuts or natural almonds
1 tablespoon freshly squeezed lemon juice
2 tablespoons fresh marjoram or oregano leaves
½ ounce pecorino cheese, shaved

In a large skillet, heat the oil over medium-high heat. Add the squash and nuts and cook, stirring frequently, until the squash is tender but not soft and the hazelnuts are toasted, about 7 minutes. Add the lemon juice and marjoram or oregano and toss to combine. Transfer to a platter and top with the pecorino cheese.

Winter

Acorn

This dark green, ribbed squash has golden yellow flesh that is dry and sweet. It's one of the best baking squashes when it's halved and topped with butter and maple syrup. The vigorous vines are productive and fruits store well over winter. First listed in seed catalogs in 1913, Acorn is also called Table Queen.

(80 to 90 Days)

Buttercup

One of the tastiest of the winter squashes, Buttercup has thick, dry flesh full of caramelized sugar, roasted chestnut, and sweet potato flavors. Popular since the 1920s, this heirloom makes delicious gourmet soups and flavorful pies.

(100 Days)

Blue Hubbard

Often mistaken for a large gourd due to it bluish gray, ribbed, and warty skin, Blue Hubbard has delicious sweet orange flesh that makes tantalizing pies. Its skin is extra thick and tough on the 5- to 10-pound fruits. You may have to hit it with a hammer to crack the rind! Obviously, it stores well. This heirloom was introduced in Marblehead, Massachusetts, in the 1700s, coming aboard sailing ships from the West Indies.

(90 to 100 Days)

Butternut

When ripe, Butternut's flesh turns increasingly deep orange, and becomes sweeter and richer. Considered one of the top ten foods for vitamin A content, Butternut's bottle-shaped, tan-colored fruits store up to 6 months. This heirloom from New England is also called Waltham Butternut.

(110 Days)

Summer

Delicata

This incredibly beautiful heirloom, first introduced in 1894, has 2-pound white fruits striped and splashed with green and orange. The deep orange flesh is super sweet and firm. Although Delicata is considered a summer squash, it can store for 3 or 4 months if it's picked when it's fully mature. Delicata is also called Peanut Squash.

(95 to 110 Days)

Black Zucchini

Black Zucchini's flavor, which is slightly sweet and fresh, remains even when the zucchini grow large. The flesh is greenish white inside the straight, black-green squash. Don't plant too many seeds, because the vigorous bushy plants are ever-bearing and produce huge numbers! Black Zucchini has been a favorite of home gardeners and farmers since 1931.

(45 to 65 Days)

Cocozelle

Another bush type, productive squash, Cocozelle has a nutty flavor and tender texture. An Italian heirloom from the 1800s, its long, slender green fruits have darker green stripes. Pick them when they're tiny for stir-fries, or when they're 6 to 8 inches long to steam or grill. Cocozelle is also called Italian Vegetable Marrow.

(55 to 65 Days)

Tromboncino

Long—up to 18 inches—and thin, Tromboncino curves into a bell shape at its blossom end, making this squash look like a trombone or question mark. The flavor is mild, its skin is tender, and most of the squash is seed-free. It's *excellent* eaten raw in salads or crudités. Pick them when they're small for best flavor and train vines upward on a trellis to increase yield. This heirloom originated in Albenga, Italy, and was introduced into the U.S. in 1863.

(50 to 60 Days)

White Patty Pan

Scalloped white squash start green, ripening to white when the flavor is at its best. Harvest White Patty Pan at about 6 inches in diameter for a sweet, nutty taste. This ancient variety was commonly grown by Native Americans who shared it with early colonists.

(55 Days)

Yellow Crookneck

Yellow Crookneck's tender yellow skin and white flesh are faintly sweet and nutty. Steam, fry, or grill for the best flavors. One of the oldest summer-type squashes, the Spanish found this heirloom in the Americas and took it back to Europe with them. Native Americans were growing Yellow Crookneck when colonists arrived over 300 years ago. Large, almost bushy vines take up a lot of room in a garden, but this variety is prolific. Keep squash picked so more will form.

(55 Days)

Pumpkin

Connecticut Field

The best pumpkin for jack-o'-lanterns is this pre-1700 Native American heirloom weighing 20 pounds or more. The rind is a deep yellowish orange, and the flesh is yellow, thick, and stringy—making it poor quality for eating. Connecticut King is excellent for livestock feed though.

(100 to 120 Days)

Long Island Cheese

High sugar levels and a deep orange flesh high in beta-carotene make Long Island Cheese *the best* pie pumpkin. Slightly flattened, buff-colored fruits range from 6 to 10 pounds. Originally grown in the New Jersey and New York areas, Long Island Cheese was first listed in seed catalogs in the early 1800s and is one of the oldest pumpkins on the market. It resembles a wheel of cheese, hence its name. The pumpkins store up to 6 months.

(90 to 100 Days)

Rouge Vif d'Etampes

Known as the "Cinderella pumpkin" because of its resemblance to the fairy tale character's magic coach, this deeply ribbed, red-orange pumpkin can grow almost big enough to hold a little princess. This French heirloom gets as large as 3 feet in diameter and 40 pounds. A highly ornamental pumpkin, Rouge Vif d'Etampes was introduced to the U.S. in the late 1800s by the W. Atlee Burpee Seed Company.

(90 to 110 Days)

Small Sugar

The rich, sweet yellow-orange flesh of Small Sugar is perfect for baking. Native Americans gave these seeds to the early colonists, who grew them as a winter food source. It was also listed in seed catalogs after 1838 as New England Pie pumpkin. Tough rinds make these small, 5-pound pumpkins ideal for storage.

(80 to 100 Days)

Chapter Sixteen

Tomatoes

There's no other way to say this: tomato flowers are promiscuous. They spread their pollen everywhere, mating with any tomato in the area. It's no surprise that new varieties arise from these casual affairs, including a completely American original, Mortgage Lifter. The first Mortgage Lifter came from William Estler of Barboursville, West Virginia. He found the tomato growing in his garden in the 1920s and thought enough of it to stabilize its genetic traits. He had a lawyer register the name Mortgage Lifter in 1932. Estler sold thousands of plants from what he believed was an accidental cross between Pritchard and Ponderosa Pink tomatoes, the only two he grew on his farm. One of his employees dubbed the fast-selling plants as "mortgage lifters," and Estler adopted the name. The original Mortgage Lifter tomato variety weighs from 1 to 3 pounds, and is low acid, sweet, and meaty with small seed cavities. And yes, it's pink.

About the same time Estler was stabilizing his variety Mortgage Lifter, M.C. Byles started his quest for the perfect tomato two counties away in Logan, West Virginia. Not a gardener, he complained to his wife Elizabeth that he disliked store-bought tomatoes. She fired back, "If the tomatoes don't suit you, then go and invent you one that does." So, he went to the library and read about breeding tomatoes. He settled on four varieties he liked and cross-pollinated them; German Johnson and Belgium Giant were probably two of the varieties used. Once he had the tomato he wanted, Byles sold plants for $1 each during the Great Depression. After he sold his first six thousand, Byles paid off his home's mortgage—hence another Mortgage Lifter.

Plump orange ones, green cherry tomatoes, fuzzy yellow salad types, chestnut brown beefsteak tomatoes—these are what the average person thinks of when they hear the words "heirloom vegetables." Tomatoes have become the stars of the heirloom world, featured on gourmet menus, temptingly stacked in organic grocery stores, and featured as the bestsellers at farmers' markets. Tomatoes are everywhere, educating consumers about how succulent, savory, and exciting heirlooms are. Tomatoes are the most widely grown vegetable worldwide, and now heirlooms have become the most sought-after ones for gardens and dinner plates, almost to the point of obsession. That's because there are so many colors, shapes, and flavors beyond the round, red, hard hybrid tomatoes we've been fed for over seventy years. Let's try some.

In the Kitchen with Doreen

Tomatoes

For the best flavor, pick the tomatoes the day you want to use them or harvest them slightly green, eating the tomatoes as they ripen.

When killing freezes threaten, pick all the green tomatoes. Place them in a single layer in cardboard boxes and store in a warm, dry area. Tomatoes will ripen within 2 to 3 months, lengthening your harvest. Think homegrown heirlooms for Christmas!

One medium-sized tomato contains half the daily recommended amount of vitamin C and one-third of vitamin A. It also has the same amount of fiber contained in a slice of whole wheat bread.

Use the end-of-season tomato glut to make freezer tomato sauce. Roast the tomatoes with their skins intact along with chunks of onion and peeled garlic cloves in a 350 degree F oven for at least 30 minutes, or until the tomatoes are soft. Cool and then purée in a food processor or blender. Add salt to taste. Italian herbs can be added if the sauce will be used for pasta dishes. Freeze in one-quart plastic containers. This freezer sauce will last up to a year.

Never ripen a tomato in direct sunlight, such as on a kitchen windowsill. It loses most of its vitamin C.

Use a bread knife or one with a serrated edge to slice tomatoes. It goes through the skin without tearing and produces perfectly thin slices.

Store tomatoes with their stem ends down to keep them longer.

To oven dry tomatoes, cut cherry, grape, or plum varieties in half; cut larger ones into ¼-inch-thick slices. Preheat an oven to 250 degrees F. Line a baking sheet with parchment and place the tomatoes, cut sides up, ½ to 1 inch apart. Salt and pepper them, adding any chopped herbs you'd like. Bake until no juices run out; about 1 hour for small tomatoes, and up to 4 hours for larger slices. The longer they oven dry, the more intense the flavor becomes. Cool completely and store in an airtight container in the refrigerator up to 3 days or freeze for up to 2 months.

Cream of Fresh Tomato Soup

Makes 5 to 6 servings

3 tablespoons extra-virgin olive oil
1½ cups chopped red onions (2 onions)
2 carrots, unpeeled, chopped
1 tablespoon minced garlic (3 cloves)
4 pounds vine-ripened tomatoes, coarsely
    chopped (5 large tomatoes)
1½ teaspoons sugar
1 tablespoon tomato paste
¼ cup packed chopped fresh basil leaves
3 cups chicken broth
1 tablespoon kosher salt
2 teaspoons freshly ground pepper
¾ cup heavy whipping cream
Julienned fresh basil leaves, for garnish
Croutons

Heat the oil in a large, heavy pot over medium-low heat. Add the onions and carrots and sauté for about 10 minutes, until very tender. Add the garlic and cook for 1 minute. Add the tomatoes, sugar, tomato paste, basil, broth, salt, and pepper and stir well. Bring the soup to a boil, lower the heat, and simmer, uncovered, for 30 to 40 minutes, until the tomatoes are very tender.

Add the cream to the soup and process it through a food mill into a bowl, discarding the dry pulp that's left. Reheat the soup over low heat just until hot and serve with the basil leaves and croutons.

Heirloom Tomato Salad

Makes 4 servings

2 cups baby lettuce leaves
1 Mortgage Lifter or Brandywine tomato
2 Green Zebra tomatoes
2 Black Prince tomatoes
Fresh basil leaves
½ cup crumbled feta cheese
Olive oil
Wine vinegar or balsamic vinegar

Divide the lettuce leaves among 4 salad plates. Slice all the tomatoes thinly and arrange them on top of the lettuce. Overlap the slices and alternate the colors. Toss the basil on top of the tomato slices. Sprinkle each salad with feta cheese. Drizzle with the oil and vinegar.

Fresh Tomato Penne

Makes 4 servings

3 cloves garlic, divided
3 fresh oregano sprigs or ¾ teaspoon
    dried oregano, divided
3 fresh rosemary sprigs or ¾ teaspoon
    dried rosemary, divided
¾ cup fresh basil leaves, julienned
2 pounds firm heirloom tomatoes, such
    as Pineapple, Mortgage Lifter, or
    Black Prince, cut into chunks
8 ounces penne pasta
Kosher salt
½ cup freshly grated Asiago cheese
¼ cup freshly grated Parmesan cheese

Mince 2 garlic cloves. Strip the leaves from 2 oregano sprigs and 2 rosemary sprigs (if using dried, use ½ teaspoon each), and chop the leaves. In a small bowl, combine the chopped garlic, chopped oregano, chopped rosemary, and basil.

Add the remaining garlic clove, oregano sprig, and rosemary sprig to a large pot of boiling water. (If using dried oregano and rosemary, add ¼ teaspoon of each.) Add the pasta and cook al dente. Drain the pasta, but do not rinse. Transfer to a serving dish and add the garlic and herb mixture, tomatoes, Asiago cheese, and Parmesan cheese. Toss to blend.

Small-Fruited and Cherry

Red Currant

These *tiny* tomatoes—four Red Currants will fit on a dime—are packed with the intense sweet-acid flavor all great tomatoes have. First found growing wild on a Peruvian beach in 1707, Red Current plants are very hardy and tomatoes will withstand light freezes.

(65 to 75 Days) Indeterminate

Small-Fruited and Cherry

Green Grape

Spicy, sweet, and juicy, these green cherry tomatoes are addictive, almost like candy, especially when eaten out of hand. A Class III heirloom created by Tom Wagner of Tater Mater Seeds in 1986, this is the only true green cherry tomato available today. It's a controlled cross between Yellow Pear and Evergreen. Each tomato is about an ounce and grows in clusters of six to twelve. Plants are tolerant of diseases and produce large crops.

(65 to 75 days) Determinate

Yellow Pear

Low-acid and sweet, these 2-ounce pear-shaped cherry tomatoes grow in clusters of seven to nine and are perfect for snacking, salads, and as garnish for entrees when halved lengthwise. Vines sprawl everywhere, so make sure plants are caged or grown against fencing where they can climb. This pre-1800s cherry-type tomato produces huge crops all season long. Thomas Jefferson grew Yellow Pear, as did most gardeners but they were used mainly for *desserts* then. To the Pennsylvania Germans, these little morsels were known as "tomato figs" and were dried, sugared, and preserved.

(70 to 80 Days) Indeterminate

Small-Fruited and Cherry

Black Prince

Black Prince's flesh is brown, juicy, and a sublime combination of sweet, salty, and wine flavors. The small, smooth 2-ounce tomatoes have garnet skins and green shoulders. Originally from Irkutsk, Russia, this heirloom grows well in cooler climates. Plants produce big crops, but they stay small and are suitable for large patio containers.

(70 to 80 Days) Indeterminate

Garden Peach

Yellow, blushed with rose, these fuzzy 2-ounce tomatoes resemble small peaches, and they almost taste like them. The flavor is fruity with a touch of acid; a peachy aroma is evident when a tomato is bit into or cut. Garden Peach stores well when they're picked green. Kids love this ancient heirloom that was grown over 3,000 years ago in Peru.

(75 to 85 Days) Indeterminate

Purple Calabash

Purplish, pleated fruits, which average 2 to 3 inches in diameter, are seedy but filled with an intense fruity Cabernet flavor with a dash of salt. Purple Calabash is extremely tolerant of drought, which further intensifies the tomato's flavor. Plants produce heavy crops that store well. Purple Calabash is possibly the oldest tomato in existence today. European herbalists grew it in the 1500s to cure madness and stimulate the libido.

(80 to 90 days) Indeterminate

Silvery Fir Tree

As the first homegrown tomato to ripen, their sprightly flavor is to be savored. Heavily dissected, carrot-top foliage on 2-foot-tall plants, as well as its earliness, set apart this Russian heirloom. Silvery Fir Tree bears fruit very early. The first medium red 3-inch tomatoes are ripe 8 weeks after setting out transplants, and the entire crop is produced within a 2 to 3 week period.

(55 to 70 Days) Determinate

Medium Size and Paste

Amish Paste

Its assertive, balanced sweet-acid taste makes Amish Paste excellent when eaten fresh or when used to make tomato paste, sauce, or salsa. Fruits are large, 8- to 12-ounces, meaty and heart-shaped. Amish Paste was discovered in Wisconsin, but originally came from Amish farmers in Pennsylvania.

(80 to 90 Days) Indeterminate

Banana Legs

A rare paste-type tomato, Banana Legs' fleshy fruits turn yellow with light green stripes that mature to orange-yellow. Its flesh is yellow, dry, sweet, and meaty—perfect for making low-acid sauces, salsas, and fresh relishes like pico de gallo. Fruits are 1½ inches wide and 4 inches long. It's another Tom Wagner selection.

(70 to 75 Days) Determinate

Medium Size and Paste

Evergreen

Even though they look unripe, Evergreen tomatoes are brimming with sweetness and fruity nuances. Tomatoes average 10 ounces, vines are vigorous and productive, plus—big bonus—the plants tolerate hot, humid climates. Evergreen looks gorgeous when served sliced with two or more other colored tomatoes such as black, yellow, and red. This old heirloom variety was introduced to modern customers by Glecklers Seedsmen around 1950. It's a popular market variety, sold in many upscale stores, and also goes by the name Emerald Evergreen.

(70 to 80 Days) Indeterminate

Green Zebra

Green Zebra is the perfect tomato for colorful salads or as a slicing tomato. Fruits ripen to chartreuse with alternating lime zebra-like stripes. Its flesh is emerald colored and rich tasting, sweet with an acid note of an aged Chardonnay. Vines are well branched and provide good foliage cover. A Class III heirloom developed by Tom Wagner in 1983, Green Zebra was chosen by chef Alice Waters to feature on her menu at Chez Panisse in Berkeley, California. Fruits are slightly elongated globes, some slightly ridged at the shoulder, averaging 3 to 5 ounces.

(78 Days) Indeterminate

Medium Size and Paste

Nebraska Wedding

Nebraska Wedding has shiny orange skin and flesh, which tastes fruity and meaty. Although the plant averages only 3 feet, cage or stake it because it's a heavy producer. Fruits of 3 to 4 inches diameter are set in clusters of three to five all over the plant. All ripen within a 20-day period. Nebraska Wedding is, ironically, most likely from Iowa.

(85 to 100 Days) Determinate

Medium Size and Paste

Schimmeig Stoo

Schimmeig Stoo's walls are thick and meaty, able to withstand stuffing with chicken or tuna salad. This low-acid tomato is mild in flavor, but it has a decidedly tomato taste, and is the perfect foil for well-seasoned fillings. Fruits weigh 5 to 8 ounces, resemble bell peppers in shape, and have four lobes sparsely filled with seeds. An artistically marbled and striped red, orange, and yellow hollow tomato, Schimmeig Stoo is a Class III heirloom created by Tom Wagner in the 1980s from four heirloom parents. He named the unique tomato to honor his maternal grandfather, J. J. Kaighin, who was born on the Isle of Mann, off the eastern coast of England in the Irish Sea. Kaighin was one of the last native speakers of the nearly dead Manx language, and Tom remembered much of it from his youth. Schimmeig Stoo literally means "striped hollow" in Manx.

(70 to 80 Days) Indeterminate

White Beauty

White Beauty tomatoes are mild, meaty, and sweet due to their high sugar content. Plants produce heavy crops of 8- to 10-ounce creamy white tomatoes. The flesh is also white and the tomato has few seeds. Thought to be extinct until recently, this unusual heirloom was introduced to American gardens between 1850 and 1863.

(80 to 85 Days) Indeterminate

Beefsteak

Brandywine

The queen of beefsteaks by which all others are measured, this highly flavored tomato is full of sweetness, robust wine notes, and salty nuances. Brandywine is probably an old Amish strain saved from generation to generation. Another theory says that the W. Atlee Burpee Seed Company introduced it in 1886 and called it Turner's Hybrid. It was not uncommon at that time for seedsmen to rename a variety to create more sales. Large, sprawling plants have leaves shaped like potato foliage. Fruits of 1 to 2 pounds have deep pink skin and red flesh. Other strains of Brandywine are available such as Red Brandywine, Black Brandywine, and Yellow Brandywine, which has an orange skin.

(75 to 90 Days) Indeterminate

Beefsteak

Black Krim

Meaty, salty, and smoky, this deep reddish brown-fleshed tomato has a full-bodied taste worth savoring. Black Krim's skin is brownish purple. The 10- to 16-ounce fruits need a long, hot summer to produce the deepest colors. In cooler climates, the skin and flesh will be paler with fewer dark tones. Its name comes from the area where it grew for centuries, the Crimean peninsula (Krim) on the Ukrainian Black Sea.

(80 to 95 Days) Indeterminate

Great White

Sweet, almost like ripe melon to the taste, this white beefsteak reminds me of a mixture of fresh pineapple, melon, and guava. Great White is aptly named; huge creamy white tomatoes weigh 14 to 16 ounces. When ripe, they have a yellowish hue on the blossom end. The plants are extremely productive and hardy, featuring a great amount of foliage to protect itself against sunscald. Great White does well in hot climates, as the plants are drought and crack resistant. This heirloom traces back to the Civil War era.

(85 Days) Indeterminate

Beefsteak

Mortgage Lifter

Saturated with bold tomato flavor, Mortgage Lifter beefsteak tomatoes deliver a juicy jolt of what a tomato should be in every bite. The plants are highly productive, disease resistant, and continue to set fruit until frost. Large—the fruits can reach 4 pounds—slightly flattened pink-red fruits are meaty and flavorful.

(80 days) Indeterminate

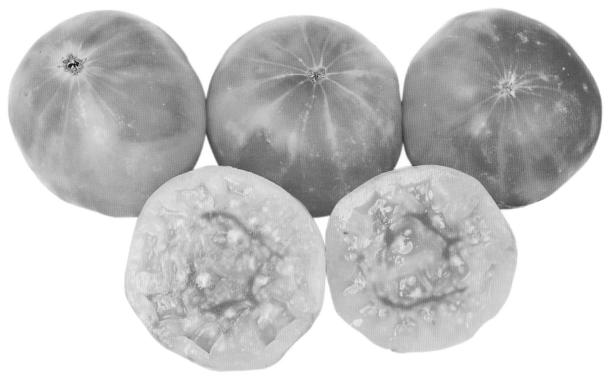

Pineapple

Not only is this huge beefsteak gorgeous—tawny gold swirled and striped with vivid red and pink—it has a big tomato perfume and taste with a fruity finish. It's my favorite tomato, especially for BLTs. The artistic stripes and swirls infuse the yellow flesh, too, with plenty of color. Fruits weigh about 2 pounds each. The vines grow vigorously and produce plenty of foliage to shade developing fruit from sunscald.

(80 to 95 Days) Indeterminate

Southern Nights

This outstanding heirloom is a rare, old, traditional Russian variety. When sliced, Southern Night's flesh is blackish red with a very rich, sweet, yet acid flavor. The skin is a dusky chestnut or red, depending on the climate. The hotter it is, the darker the colors. The potato-leaf determinate plants produce large crops of 10-ounce fruits that ripen within a 2-week period. This one grows well in hot, humid climates.

(80 to 85 Days) Determinate

Fruits

Chapter Eighteen

Apples, Pears, and Asian Pears

Scraggly apple trees with little, tart fruits grew wild in the rugged Tien Shan mountains of eastern Kazakstan in 8,000 B.C. They were carried throughout the world by merchants traveling the Old Silk Road and by invading armies. Most of the apple varieties in the United States are European imports, even the ones the first colonists found growing on the shores of what is now Maine. According to George Stilphen, author of *The Apples of Maine*, many trees came to the islands along the coast in the 1500s, long before the colonists. European fishermen traveled farther and farther west, setting up permanent camps on the Maine islands where the waters teamed with fish. They brought their families and the plants of their home countries to produce food for the months they lived on the islands. Their apple trees migrated inland and native tribes cultivated them. That's why the Pilgrims thought that numerous apple varieties were native to North America.

Pears are just as fascinating. These buttery, sweet fruits are true heirlooms, greatly exceeding the "any variety in existence before 1900" rule that defines an antique fruit. Varieties like Bartlett, Comice, Bosc, and Anjou had their origins in fifteenth through nineteenth century England, France, and Germany. Why have these ancient pear varieties persevered? They have terrific flavor (a good balance of sweetness and undertones), and they have what is known as "melting flesh." That's a buttery feel on the tongue and firm flesh that is soft to bite.

Asian pears migrated to the West Coast in the late 1800s from China, Japan, and Korea. Their texture relies on grit cells for the crunchy, juicy, coarse mouth feel that defines the huge pears' prized taste. Asian pears bruise easily because of their juiciness and won't store for long, so they're usually eaten out of hand. Their large size and unique, aromatic appearance give the Asian pear a cachet with consumers. Just one taste of any of the featured apples, pears or Asian pears in this chapter will make an heirloom convert of anyone!

In the Kitchen with Doreen

Apples, Pears, and Asian Pears

Apples ripen ten times faster at room temperature than they do when refrigerated or stored in a cold basement or root cellar.

Thaw frozen pie dough or a puff pastry sheet, and roll it into an 8- by 12-inch rectangle. Place it on a greased cookie sheet. Pinch the sides of the pastry to form a low rim. Then slice your favorite apples, such as Esopus Spitzenburg or Cox's Orange Pippin, and arrange the slices in an overlapping pattern all over the pastry. Sprinkle apples with a mixture of brown sugar, cinnamon, and nutmeg. Bake about 25 minutes at 350 degrees F or until the crust is brown. Cool slightly before cutting into pieces. Serve warm for a fast, *heavenly* apple harvest treat.

Cut a couple of slits in apples for baking so that skins don't wrinkle and pull away from the flesh.

Most of the vitamin C in Asian and European pears is in the skin.

To quickly ripen a pear, put it in a paper bag with an apple overnight. Apples give off ethylene gas, which ripens pears and many vegetables, such as tomatoes.

Because Asian pears are picked when they're ripe, refrigerate them immediately. They last about 60 days before their skins start to shrivel.

Dry Asian pear slices in a food dehydrator for later use. Store slices in sealed plastic bags or containers. Dried slices make sweet, tasty snacks or can be soaked in warm water for an hour to rehydrate them for salads.

Southern Waldorf Salad

Makes 6 servings

2 tablespoons orange juice
3 large tart red apples, cored,
    unpeeled, diced
½ cup diced celery
½ cup sour cream
½ cup raisins
¼ cup chopped pecans or walnuts
1½ teaspoons sugar
Lettuce leaves (optional)

In a large bowl, sprinkle the orange juice over the apples. Toss gently and drain. Return the apples to the bowl. Add the celery, sour cream, raisins, nuts, and sugar and stir well. Cover and chill. Serve on lettuce leaves, if desired.

Sara's Apple Pie

Makes 8 servings

1 cup sugar
½ cup orange juice
1 stick butter
4 cups peeled and sliced apples
1 double piecrust, unbaked

Preheat the oven to 350 degrees F.

Add the sugar, orange juice, and butter to a saucepan and cook over medium heat until slightly thickened. Add the apples to the mixture and cook until tender. Transfer the apples to the piecrust, top with the remaining crust, and bake for 50 minutes or until golden brown. (If the crust is browning too fast, cover with foil.)

Poached Pears

Makes 8 servings

Zest of 1 lemon, in strips
1 cinnamon stick, halved
¼ teaspoon ground allspice
¼ teaspoon freshly ground pepper
4 cups apple cider, fresh if possible
1 cup water
8 Bosc pears, peeled and cored
    (from the bottom)

In a large heavy pan, combine the lemon zest, cinnamon stick, allspice, pepper, and cider, and water. Add the pears. Simmer, turning the pears occasionally, until the pears are easily pierced with the tip of a knife but before they fall apart, about 20 minutes. Remove the pears to a serving bowl. Boil the cider mixture in the pan until syrupy, about 15 minutes. Discard the cinnamon sticks. Pour the syrup over the pears and refrigerate until ready to serve.

Apple

Ashmead's Kernel

Ashmead's Kernel's strong, sugary-sharp cider flavor sets this mid-season heirloom apart from any other apples. There are undertones of spice and honey too. Its skin is russeted and golden brown. These apples store well, up to 6 months. Ashmead's Kernel is prone to cedar apple rust disease, so bag them for perfect fruit. It was first raised in 1700 by Gloucester, England, physician Dr. Ashmead. This is my favorite apple.

Cox's Orange Pippin

The flavor of Cox's Orange Pippin is described by many as spicy, honeyed, nutty, and pear-like, in subtle blends. Flavor combinations can change by the bite or the apple. It's often praised as the ultimate dessert apple to be eaten out of hand. Bred in England in 1825 by Richard Cox, a retired brewer, this variety took the American market by a storm in the late 1800s. Trees are disease-prone so bag apples to harvest perfect fruit. Diseases are fewer and production is higher in cooler summer climates.

Calville Blanc D'Hiver

Rich, sweet-sharp aromatic flavor makes this heirloom the perfect apple for the classic French dessert *Tarte aux Pommes* and for eating out of hand. Calville Blanc D'Hiver originated in the Alsace-Lorraine region of France in 1598. Pale green in color with light red dots on the side exposed to the sun, it turns yellow in storage as it matures. Apples should be stored a month or longer to develop their maximum flavor. The trees are naturally small, and harvests are light—but it is so worth it. This heirloom needs a hot summer to develop its best flavor.

Apple

Esopus Spitzenburg

Biting into an Esopus Spitzenburg produces an *explosion* of flavors. The hard, crisp yellow flesh is filled with the flavor and perfume of rich, fruity acidity. Russet dots cover its brilliant orange-red skin. It's the ultimate gourmet apple. This heirloom came from Esopus, New York, in 1790 and was Thomas Jefferson's favorite dessert apple. Apples can be stored for months and still retain their flavor.

Lady Apples

Small, slightly acid yet sweet, these perfumed apples are borne in clusters. Sweetness builds during storage and the acid components decline. Lady Apple's bright red coloring, with white, fine-grained flesh, makes these tiny apples as pretty as they are tasty. Trees are small and prone to cedar apple rust. The Lady Apple is the oldest apple variety in existence today and was grown by the Romans. Because of its size and flavor, ladies during the Renaissance would keep one tucked in their bosoms and take it out to freshen their breath. This variety is also called Roman, Api, and the Christmas apple due to its late ripening. It's traditionally been used in Wassail bowls, as stocking stuffers, and in centerpieces.

Sheep's Nose

Unusually aromatic, some find the perfume of Sheep's Nose peculiar. Its aroma and taste are slightly sweet with intense cinnamon notes. The thin, tender skin can turn a dark purple in the right growing conditions, and its flesh is creamy white and becomes dry with time. Eat these aromatic apples out of hand soon after harvesting. They are excellent for drying and baking, holding their shape and flavor in pies. This variety is thought to have originated in the early 1800s; it is also called Black Gilliflower. The name came from its shape, which resembles the elongated nose of a sheep.

Wolf River

Wolf River's coarsely textured flesh is slightly tart, soft, juicy, and cream-colored. These *huge* apples (they range from 16 to 30 ounces) are best cooked, making them excellent in pies, crisps, and cobblers. Because of their size, it will only take one or two apples to make a pie. Trees are scab and mildew resistant and are very winter hardy. A true American antique apple, Wolf River was discovered in 1850 along the Wolf River in Freemont, Wisconsin.

Pear

Anjou

Anjou pears are large and light green. The flesh is aromatic, juicy, and sweet with citrus notes. For the best taste, store this nineteenth century French heirloom in the refrigerator for a month or two after harvesting. Also called D'Anjou, this pear's puree is used by Jelly Belly® to make their Juicy Pear flavor of jelly beans.

Comice

Often referred to as the best pear variety, Comice is extra juicy, with no grit, and spicy sweet. Bred in France about 1850, this heirloom derives its name from the phrase *doyenne du comice*, meaning, "top of the show." Trees need regular pruning to keep them small.

Flemish Beauty

Flemish Beauty pears are sweet and aromatic with a musky flavor. The flesh is firm, but tender, becoming meltingly soft when they're ripe. This one is good for eating out of hand and pairs well with strong cheeses, nuts, and red wines. It grows well in cold climates and doesn't require a pollinator. Flemish Beauty was first grown in 1810 in New York.

Pear

Bosc

Eat this Belgium heirloom before it is fully ripe for the best flavor, which is spicy and sugary. The flesh of a Bosc pear is dense and crunchy. Its skin is heavily russeted in cinnamon brown tones. This heirloom came to the U.S. in the 1830s. It's also called Kaiser.

Forelle

Strongly flavored and sweetly astringent, this German heirloom has a discernible cinnamon spiciness. Forelle is one of the smallest pear varieties and can almost be called miniature; the fruits are about 3 inches high. Forelle is best eaten when it's still firm; when ready to eat, the greenish skin turns a brilliant yellow. Native to northern Saxony in Germany since the 1600s, Forelle translates as "trout" from German.

Seckel

Different from other pears, Seckel is intensely sweet and crunchy. It's thought to be a cross between a pear and an Asian pear, and was discovered around 1820 in Pennsylvania. A small pear, this heirloom takes longer to ripen than other pears, but it stores well in the refrigerator.

Asian Pears

Chojuro

Chojuro has slightly gritty, crispy white flesh packed with aromatic butterscotch flavor. Pick these large russeted fruits when they first turn yellow-brown to avoid skin discoloration and bruising later. Discovered in Japan in 1895, this heirloom has high sugar content and stores well, up to 6 months. Trees are precocious, meaning they bear early, usually their second season in the ground. They are self-fruitful, but set a heavier crop if another pear or Asian pear is planted nearby.

20th Century

The large, round yellow-skinned fruit of 20th Century is crunchy, juicy, and sweet without being cloying. It matures early: July in hot temperature climates and late August in northern areas like Wisconsin. Trees are self-fruitful, meaning they need no other variety to pollinate it. This is the type of Asian pear you are mostly likely to see in grocery stores. Its fruit keeps up to 6 months in storage such as the refrigerator. Also called Nijisseiki, this heirloom originated in Japan about 1900.

Growing Your Own Isn't Difficult

Hands down, apples, pears, and Asian pears are the most pesticide- and fungicide-laden foods grown commercially. Orchards start spraying trees in late winter and continue, sometimes weekly, until fruit is harvested five to eight months later—all in the name of producing perfect apples and pears without blemishes. It's what we consumers demand—defect-free, flawless fruit. Until heirloom varieties became available at farmers' markets, fruit stands, and in specialty food catalogs within the last twenty years, taste didn't matter to most people. But after you've eaten an antique apple like Cox's Orange Pippin, known for its acid-sweet complexity, or taken a bite out of a sugary Comice pear, you want more than cosmetic perfection—you want flavor. That's what antique apples, pears, and Asian pears offer—intense flavors brimming with spiciness and even nut undertones.

But growing your own isn't that difficult, even if you only have a postage-stamp-sized yard. Plenty of antique varieties are grafted onto dwarfing rootstock, and the resulting trees stay under 12 feet in height. Some varieties on M27 rootstock don't grow any bigger than a shrub, about 6 feet tall and wide.

Another thing to note is that all apples need another variety to pollinate their flowers. Golden Delicious, which can be found on dwarf rootstock, is an excellent pollinator of any antique variety. Pears and Asian pears will pollinate each other. Even the ornamental pears that bloom prodigiously in spring will pollinate both types of pears.

DWARF ROOTSTOCKS

Not all dwarfing rootstocks are alike; they can produce mature trees that range from a petite 5 or 6 feet to 20 feet tall. You also want to pick the rootstock that fits your climate. So be an educated consumer—know what you are buying to select the antique apple or pear tree that suits your needs. This chart lists recommended rootstocks and notes the average height a tree grafted to that rootstock will grow, as well as hardiness zones and other notes.

APPLES

Bud 9: 8 feet; very cold hardy; Zones 3 to 5

M9: 8 to 10 feet; tolerates wet soils; Zones 5 to 8 (protect roots with snow cover in colder areas)

M7: 16 to 18 feet; tolerates wet soils; Zones 6 to 8

M26: 10 to 14 feet; very cold hardy; Zones 3 to 5

M27: 6 to 8 feet; requires extra moisture so irrigate often; Zones 5 to 8

MM106: 10 to 12 feet; excellent for hot climates; Zones 8 to 10

M111: 15 to 20 feet; drought tolerant; moderately cold hardy; Zones 4 to 8

PEARS AND ASIAN PEARS

OHXF33: 10 to 16 feet; easily kept smaller with summer pruning; cold-hardy; bears fruit after a year or two (in-ground); Zones 4 to 8

OHXF51: 8 to 12 feet; the best rootstock for hot, humid climates; Zones 6 to 9

Quince: 4 to 10 feet; significantly dwarfs pear trees; compatible only with Comice, Anjou, and Seckel pears; best for hot, humid climates with clay soils; not cold-hardy; Zones 7 to 9

The Importance of Grafting

The terms "grafted" and "rootstock" may be unfamiliar to you, especially if you've never grown fruit trees. But all tree fruit varieties, even newer ones developed in the last thirty years, are grafted on rootstock so that they bear a crop sooner and are automatically adapted to the local climate. A tree growing from its own roots may lose its entire root system at temperatures below zero and die, or it could die from root rot and other fungal diseases prevalent in hot, humid climates. Adapted rootstocks prevent these things from happening, and the grafted tree flourishes. Grafting is done by binding together the cut ends of the rootstock and a small length of desired tree branch that has at least four fat, healthy buds. Usually, cuts are made on a diagonal and matched to fit. Sometimes, if the variety cutting is small and the rootstock is large, a notch is cut in the rootstock and the cutting is inserted. No matter the technique, the graft is then sealed with melted wax and wrapped with grafting, masking, or even duct tape. There's plenty of information available on grafting, and County Extension Services teach classes in grafting. Thankfully for those of us with little time or manual dexterity, a number of mail-order nurseries carry antique fruit trees grafted to the appropriate rootstock for your area. See the Resources section for a list.

An Ounce of Planning is Worth a Gallon of Pesticides

After you plant an antique variety of fruit tree, plan ahead to produce perfect, blemish-free fruit bursting with flavor without all those pesticides and fungicides found on grocery-store fruit. Spray dormant oil on trees in late winter, on a day when it's above 45 degrees F and when the nighttime temperature doesn't fall below 32 degrees F. Repeat dormant oil spray when buds start to swell on the trees in early spring. Then use barrier methods to protect fruit instead of insecticide and fungicide sprays. You reduce your labor and costs significantly, and you grow healthy, organic fruit that ripens a week or two earlier than normal. Soft-fleshed fruits like pears, peaches, and plums can be shielded from insect and disease damage by draping the tree with netting after fruit has set and been thinned. Fine, white organza (the same material used to make bridal veils) is available at fabric stores and is cheaper and easier to put on trees and store than fruit netting. Hard fruits like apples can be bagged. This 100-year-old Japanese technique employs little plastic bags put over developing fruit to prevent disfigurement by insects and diseases like apple cedar rust. Growers first used tiny silk bags they sewed until the 1960s when plastic bags became readily available. Apples are prized gifts in Japanese culture, selling for as much as $10 each. Perfection is a must for growers, so each apple is bagged when the fruit clusters are thinned. Bagging also works on Asian pears, despite their high water content. Soft pears rot in enclosed bags, though, because they have thin, tender skin that splits, and soft pears are full of water that cultivates fungi.

HOW TO BAG DEVELOPING FRUIT

1. Buy zipper-lock or sliding-lock 1-quart plastic bags. Snip off the two bottom corners of each bag diagonally. This allows accumulated moisture to drain away from developing fruit.
2. When set fruit is about the size of a pea, thin clusters to space apples at least 6 inches apart on branches and Asian pears at least 10 inches.
3. Place a bag over each fruit and close the zipper or slide lock around the fruit stem. If the fruit falls off during the process, it wasn't fully pollinated and would abort on its own later anyway.

After bagging, there is nothing else to do, other than to observe the developing fruit periodically. Extra heat gathered by the plastic bag will help to build the Brix level (sugar content) of apples and Asian pears and contributes to larger size. When it's time to harvest, simply snap off apples from trees as you would normally. Many growers leave apples in their bags for long-term storage, so the fruits don't dehydrate. Apples stored this way will remain crunchy and sweet much longer than those stored in a cool basement. Asian pears and apples mature a week or two earlier when grown in bags, which is a bonus in colder climates.

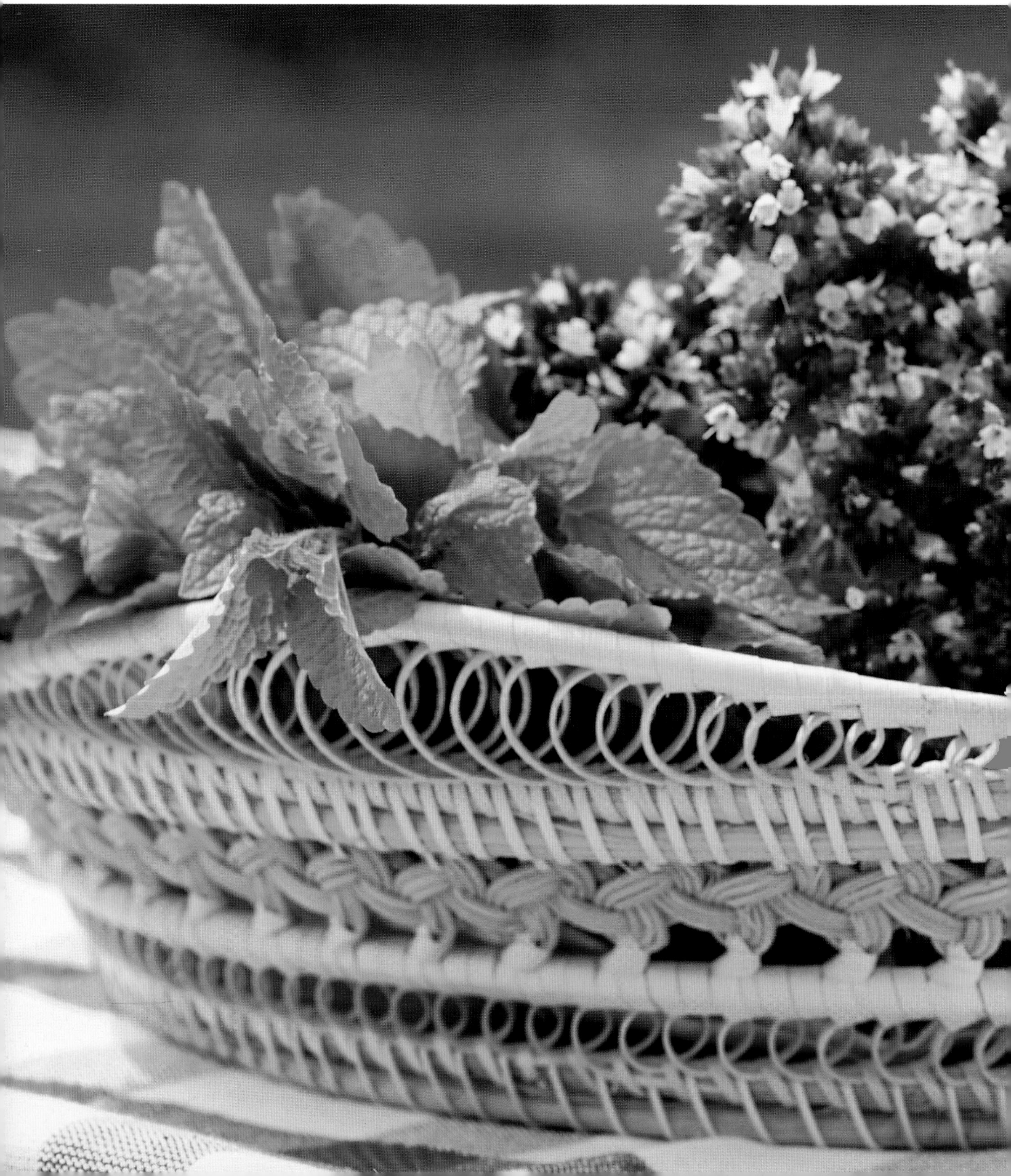

Herbs and Edible Flowers

Chapter Seventeen

Herbs and Edible Flowers

Herbs have been used since prehistoric times for curing madness and maladies, preserving food, purifying the air, and anointing leaders. Carbon dating traces cave drawings of herbs in France to 25,000 B.C. Early humans were attracted to the aromas of herbs—they rubbed strong-smelling leaves on their bodies to hide their human scent from the animals they were hunting. The Romans, and later northern Europeans, used dill to cleanse the foul air in houses during winter. Along with the Greeks, the Romans crowned their leaders with wreaths fashioned from thyme, dill, and laurel to protect them from treachery, poison, and evil spirits.

The famous Greek physician Hippocrates collected an arsenal of nearly 400 herbs for healing. He used anise to treat coughs, an ingredient still used in cough drops today. During the Middle Ages, herbs were used to preserve meat, as well as hide the taste of foods that had gone bad. However, during this time of intellectual stagnation, herbs for medicinal purposes were banned. Herbalists and some physicians were punished as witches and pagans. Many witch hunts occurred throughout Europe, but herbalism was not abandoned; it was practiced in secrecy.

Most herbs available today are the same varieties that grew 25,000 years ago. Little has been done to hybridize them, as their essential oils (which give herbs their flavor) and medicinal properties are valued. Basil and lavender are exceptions because plant breeding has made it possible for wider climate adaptation and added nuanced flavors. Jim Long, herb expert and owner of Long Creek Herbs in Blue Eye, Missouri, says basil and lavender are number one and two on consumer popularity surveys.

Many ready-to-use herbs are widely available in farmers' markets and in grocery store produce sections. Annual herbs can easily be grown from seed, but they are also commonly available as starter plants. Perennial herbs are best bought as starter plants. Many tender perennial and annual herbs can be grown in a sunny windowsill indoors during winter. Pot up an assortment and give your food a fresh kick of flavor even if there's snow on the ground!

In the Kitchen with Doreen

Herbs and Edible Flowers

Herbs, with the exception of lavender, are their most flavorful just before they flower. Harvest after the morning dew dries.

When making lavender or basil vinegars, use the flowers rather than the leaves. Flowers contain more flavor-rich oils.

Candy lavender flowers quickly by rolling them in superfine sugar after they are picked. Let flowers sit in the sugar for 48 hours, and then sift away the excess. Store them in a sealed container in a dry, dark spot. Sprinkle candied lavender on cakes, scones, trifles, or mousse for an artistic, flavorful extra.

To cure bad breath, chew a few mint leaves.

An easy way to dry any herb is to place about two cups of it in a paper grocery bag, fold over the bag top, and secure with a clothespin or other bag clip. Put the bags in the trunk of your car and close the lid. Every day or two, shake the bags to prevent the herbs from settling. Check after a week to see if herbs are fully dried. If not, leave them in the trunk a few more days.

Store dried herbs in sealed glass jars in a dark place. They can be frozen too.

Use chopped garlic chives in place of minced garlic cloves in fresh dishes such as pasta, tuna, and green salads for a milder taste.

Don't dry cilantro for later use; its flavor is greatly diminished. But you can freeze leaves to have flavorful salsas and Thai stir-fries in January! Also, harvest cilantro before it flowers; after it does, the leaves become bitter.

Dried rosemary leaves are sharp and prickly in the mouth if they're left whole. Either wrap them in cheesecloth or grind them with a mortar and pestle before adding to any dish.

Use those gorgeous blue rosemary flowers in salads or as garnish. Larger sprigs can be used as skewers for fish or shrimp shish-kabobs. For even more flavor, throw a couple of sprigs on the coals when grilling.

Blender Pesto

Makes enough for 6 servings of pasta

2 cups fresh basil leaves
½ cup olive oil
2 tablespoons pine nuts
2 cloves garlic
1 teaspoon salt
½ cup freshly grated Parmesan cheese
3 tablespoons butter, softened

Put the basil, oil, pine nuts, garlic, and salt in a blender or food processor and process at high speed until evenly blended.

Transfer to a bowl and blend in the Parmesan cheese and butter by hand. Before serving over pasta, mix in 1 or 2 tablespoons of the hot water in which the pasta was cooked.

Olive Oil and Balsamic Vinegar Herbed Dipping Sauce

Makes 1 cup

½ cup extra-virgin olive oil
¼ cup balsamic vinegar
½ teaspoon crushed red pepper flakes
1 teaspoon mashed garlic cloves
¼ teaspoon salt (optional)
1 tablespoon finely chopped fresh flat-leaf
    parsley
1 tablespoon finely chopped fresh basil

Combine all the ingredients in a small bowl and chill for 4 hours. Serve as a dipping sauce for bread or vegetables.

Lavender Tea Biscuits

Makes 24 cookies

3 sticks butter, softened
⅔ cup granulated sugar
¼ cup sifted confectioners' sugar
6 tablespoons finely chopped fresh lavender
3 teaspoons grated lemon zest
2½ cups all-purpose flour
½ cup cornstarch
¼ teaspoon salt

In a medium bowl, cream together the butter and sugars until light and fluffy. Mix in the lavender and lemon zest. In a separate medium bowl, combine the flour, cornstarch, and salt. Mix the flour mixture into the butter mixture until well blended. Divide the dough into two balls, wrap in plastic wrap, and flatten to a 1-inch thickness. Chill until firm, about 1 hour.

Preheat the oven to 325 degrees F.

On a lightly floured surface, roll the dough out to a ¼-inch thickness. Cut into shapes with cookie cutters. Place on baking sheets.

Bake for 18 to 20 minutes, until the cookies just begin to brown at the edges. Cool for a few minutes on the baking sheets, then transfer to wire racks to cool completely.

Herbs

Cilantro & Coriander

The fresh, pungent, grassy-flavored leaves that define Mexican salsas and curries from Southeast Asia are cilantro; the dried seeds of the same plant are coriander. They are the basic flavor components of pickling spices and are ground for cakes, sweet breads, and heavy puddings. A cool-season plant, harvest cilantro's dark green leaves before days turn warm for the best flavor. At about 80 degrees F, plants form large, umbrella-like flowers. Wait until coriander seeds are golden brown to harvest them. Don't dry cilantro leaves; more than 85 percent of the flavor is lost. Instead, freeze leaves in sealed bags. This heirloom has been grown as long ago as 1,500 B.C.

Gigante d'Italia Parsley

This Northern Italian heirloom has large, flat, deep green leaves packed with sweet, piquant flavors. Vigorous and robust, Gigante grows as tall as 3 feet and is one of the oldest flat-leaf parsleys. It's also called Italian Flat Leaf. Note: curled-leaf types have little flavor but are the parsley of choice for garnishing foods.

Lettuce Leaf Basil

Lettuce Leaf basil has the largest leaf of any basil, up to 6 inches long on 18-inch-high plants. The flavor is sweet and spicy. The flowers are edible, too, with an intense flavor, making them perfect for salads, sauces, and vinegars. Wrap fish or chicken kabobs with fresh leaves and grill for a tantalizing entrée. This heirloom has been around since the late 1800s. It's slow to bolt in warm weather, but keep flowers picked off to lengthen leaf production.

Genovese Sweet Basil

Genovese is the basil of choice for making pesto because of its plentiful, large perfumed leaves that are packed with sweetness and hints of clove. Genovese basil was considered a sign of love in Italy. Legend says that when a woman put a pot of this herb on her windowsill, it was a sign that she was ready to receive suitors.

Thai Basil

Unlike European basils, Asian types like Thai *gain* flavor when they flower and exude a haunting perfume of honey laced with licorice or anise. Its flavor is distinctive, with the same notes of licorice and honey that give depth to the curry, pho, and stir-fry dishes that comprise a large part of Southeast Asian cuisine. The plants and flowers are gorgeous—deep purple stems are covered with lush blooms ranging in color from lavender to merlot. This ancient herb grows wild in Thailand, Vietnam, Cambodia, Laos, and parts of Indonesia.

Herbs

Oregano

Often called the pizza herb, oregano leaves are loaded with oils that impart a strong, balsamic, bitter aroma and taste. Dry leaves for a couple days to lessen some of its bitterness. A perennial, oregano plants spread from their roots, much like mint, and can be invasive. White or pinkish purple flower spikes appear in late summer on the mounding, spreading plants. Cultivated in France since the Middle Ages, oregano is also an important herb in Mediterranean cooking.

Garlic Chives

This common chive relative has broad, flat leaves loaded with the aroma and taste of garlic, backed with a bit of sweetness. An ancient Asian perennial that grows best outdoors, garlic chive plants spread from rhizomes and often form tiny bulbs along the underground stems. White blooms on woody stems appear in late summer. Break them off so seeds don't blow and grow elsewhere. Plants go dormant in winter and are very cold hardy.

Marjoram

Related botanically to oregano, marjoram has a sweet, pine flavor that's similar to, but much gentler than, its relative. Marjoram plants are smaller and more cold sensitive than oregano. The leaves hold their flavor and perfume when dried much better than oregano does. Used by ancient civilizations as medicine, the Egyptians used the herb to embalm their pharaohs.

Thyme

The herb's flavor is much like a mild sage, but it can have underlying notes ranging from lemon to nutmeg. Growing conditions and plant mutations contribute to the differences in taste, but the overwhelming flavor is sage. A perennial, thyme plants stay small and work well to edge herb gardens or even perennial beds. Ancient Greeks named the herb *thymon*, which means "to fumigate" in Greek. They burned it to cleanse the air in foul-smelling dwellings.

Rosemary

Used to flavor food since pre-Biblical times, this evergreen shrub imparts a sweet mint/pine flavor to foods. Its perfume is the same and is used for baths, herbal oils, and potpourri. Crush the needlelike leaves to release its flavors and aromas. A tender perennial, hardy only to about Zone 7, pot up rosemary and bring indoors for the winter.

Herbs

Vietnamese Mint

Harvest the bright green leaves of this mint while it's young to enjoy its strong mint/lemon taste and perfume. It's intense and can be enjoyed from 20 to 30 feet away. Add fresh leaves to hot or cold teas, lemonade, or seltzer for a refreshing hot-day drink. Traditional Thai cuisine dishes like pho and spring rolls are enhanced by Vietnamese mint's burst of flavors. It grows wild all over the mountains and valleys of Vietnam, Thailand, and Cambodia. Plants aren't hardy beyond Zone 8 though, so grow them in a container and bring indoors for winter. This ancient mint is also called Kinh Gioi.

Hidcote Lavender

The purest, most intense lavender scent of numerous varieties, Hidcote's flowers are steam-distilled to make the oil that scented most perfumes and soaps of yesterday and today. The flowers, full of complicated sweet citrus, floral, and piney essences, impart their taste nicely to whipped cream and sugared fruits. Hidcote is a small plant, only about a foot in height, but its concentrated fragrance and deep blue flowers make it the lavender that's most planted. It's also cold hardy— most of the others aren't. With a thick mulch covering it, Hidcote has endured my minus 25 degree F winters.

Elephant's Head Amaranth

Stately (up to 9 feet), with stunning burgundy flowers, this 1800s heirloom from Germany is a relative of lamb's quarter. The new growth tips, tinged red, taste like sweet spinach and can be lightly steamed or used in salads. But it's the seeds harvested from mature flowers that provide amaranth flour, a popular gluten-free, nutritious substitute for wheat flour. Each plant produces 40,000 to 60,000 tiny seeds that can be ground into flour. I use my electric coffee mill and grind enough to use fresh to make low-carbohydrate bread. Store seeds in the refrigerator up to 6 months to preserve their nutrient-rich fat content. Ground amaranth seed, mixed with milk and honey, is a popular Mexican hot drink called atole. Cinnamon and chocolate are added to some versions of it.

Mexican Mint Marigold

It looks like a marigold plant with small yellow blooms, but its tarragon scent is powerful. Often called Mexican tarragon, the leaves have even more tarragon flavor than tarragon! Licorice and anise flavors are nearly overwhelming. A tender perennial, most gardeners grow Mexican mint marigold as an annual. It's attractive and tough, taking drought, heat, humidity, and floods in stride. Harvest the flowers to jazz up the flavors of tuna or chicken salad. The herb was grown for centuries by the Aztecs.

Crosnes

A member of the mint family, these perennial plants grow lushly throughout summer and look somewhat like spearmint. They spread on underground rhizomes and are attractive groundcovers. Dig up the pearly white tubers, which look like tiny Michelin men or miniature Nautilus shells, in fall when foliage browns. They taste like water chestnuts and can be used similarly. Add them to salads and dress with fruit vinaigrettes, such as pear-hazelnut. The grooves in the little tubers catch sauces easily. Store in the refrigerator in sealed containers for up to 3 months. Crosnes came from Peking, China, to France in 1882. They were grown near the town of Crosnes and acquired its name.

In the Market and In the Garden

In the Market

Farmers' markets are wonderful places to find heirloom edibles. Since 1994, the number of them has escalated from 1,700 to more than 6,200 in 2011, according to the United States Department of Agriculture. Their expansion has been driven by cooks and gardeners who want locally grown produce that is fresh and full of flavor. That's why so many heirlooms are featured at markets. I regularly shop one of the largest in country, the Dane County Farmers' Market in Madison, Wisconsin, for heirlooms I don't grow or never have seen, like morel mushrooms in the spring or huitlacoche (corn smut) in late summer. I'm bumping elbows with plenty of chefs from four and five-star restaurants in the Chicago, Milwaukee, and Madison areas. They're picky about the produce they buy, and I've learned from them exactly which vegetables, fruits, and herbs should go home with me. Here are some tips for you:

What to Look For

Bean: Buy string and filet beans that are young and tender, 6 inches long or less. Dried beans (in shells or shelled) should be thoroughly dry and glossy.

Beet & Swiss Chard: Ideally, choose small beets about 2 inches in diameter with their greens intact and no worm holes. Use the greens for salads and garnish. For Swiss chard, the smaller leaves are tender and mild in flavor.

Cabbage: Look for heavy heads with tightly wrapped leaves.

Broccoli: Look for firm, dense, dark green heads; those are the tastiest and most nutritious.

Cauliflower: The best cauliflower have vibrantly colored, tight curds, and heavy heads.

Kohlrabi: Look for small ones with stems less than 2 inches in diameter for the sweetest and most tender globes. Larger ones are woody, and can turn bitter.

Brussels Sprouts: Buy the smaller sprouts; they're the sweetest.

Carrot: In spring, select carrots that are the freshest looking. Pick hard, well-colored carrots in autumn for storage.

Corn: When choosing corn, look for ears with tight husks, light-colored tassels, and fresh-cut stems.

Cucumber: Pick cucumbers that have firm, unblemished skin with no yellow coloring (unless it's a yellow-skinned variety).

Eggplant: Select eggplants with shiny, tight skin that are heavy for their size.

Lettuce: Look for lettuce with crisp, moist leaves and damp, white stem cuts, not brown ones, which indicate age.

Melon: When selecting a melon other than a watermelon, look for a callused stem end that shows the melon separated from the vine on its own when it was ripe. A melon should feel heavy and have a fruity aroma. Watermelons have no perfume when they're ripe. Watermelon stems may be intact; look for a rich yellow bottom spot where the melon sat on the ground.

Onion & Garlic: Select green onions with fresh green tops and firm white roots. Onions and garlic should be firm and have several layers of scaling dried skin. Look for garlic heads with tightly packed cloves.

Peas: The tastiest peas have a fresh, shiny green look with a bit of softness. Hard, dull fresh peas are past their prime and will be starchy. Snow pea pods should be flat and shiny, but pick sugar snaps with glossy, well-filled pods.

Peppers: Sweet peppers should have smooth, shiny skins, be highly colored, and firm. The same criteria are true for hot peppers, but look for cracks around the stem end for the best flavor and heat.

Potato: Choose potatoes that are hard, with no sprouted eyes. Reject ones with green skins or spots; they are toxic.

Radish: Brightly colored with the greens still attached is a sign of freshly harvested radishes.

Squash & Pumpkin: Dried stems and rinds that cannot be pierced by a fingernail indicate winter squash and pumpkin have developed their full flavor and can be stored. With summer squash, the smaller, the better; they will be tender, sweet, and bursting with flavor.

Tomato: Luckily, many vendors offer tomato samples for tasting. Purchase those you like the best. Look for firm fruit that is deeply colored and heavy for its size. Pass up soft ones that leak liquid.

Apple: Choose firm, well-colored apples with no insect damage.

Pear: Press at the neck, near the stem; if the pear gives slightly, is is mature and sweet.

Asian Pear: Select firm, fully colored Asian pears with no green streaks. Their stems should be intact.

Herbs & Edible Flowers: Look for vibrant leaves and fresh-looking stems with no flowers or buds, which give an herb a bitter flavor. The exception to this is lavender: you want tight buds on lavender.

In the Garden

Beans

• Soak seeds overnight in warm water before planting to speed germination.

• Plant bush beans when the ground temperature is at least 60 degrees F or when the dandelions and wild violets bloom. Plant pole bean seeds 2 weeks later. Cool soil reduces germination and slows early rapid growth.

• Beans are legumes and have rhizobia bacteria on their roots that process nitrogen from the air for plant growth. Don't add manure, compost, or nitrogen fertilizer to soil; all you'll get for your trouble are large plants and no beans.

• Bean roots add nitrogen to the soil so plant nitrogen "hogs" such as squash, melons, and cucumbers next to them.

• For maximum production from bush beans, plant them intensively on 2-inch centers (2 inches apart in all directions). The plants support one another and smother sprouting weeds. Harvesting stimulates more production, so pick beans every day so plants produce more.

• When bean plants finish producing, cut them off at the ground rather than pulling them up. Bean roots, full of nitrogen-fixing bacteria nodules, will remain in the soil and feed the next crop.

Beets and Swiss Chard

• Soak Swiss chard seeds in water for 24 hours before planting. Each seed is actually a dried fruit with 1 to 5 seeds in it. Most will sprout, so it's important to thin seedlings at least to 12 inches apart so plants grow vigorously.

• For small beets to pickle, sow seeds closely, and thin to about 2 inches apart. Spaced closely, they will reach an edible size faster due to competition for nutrients and sunlight.

• Beets can be grown in shady areas of the garden and underneath taller vegetables such as tomatoes and corn. They need only 5 to 6 hours of daily direct sun. Swiss chard can also tolerate shade.

• Keep beets and Swiss chard watered during dry periods so they don't bolt, which means they send up a premature flower stalk to create seed. Flavor isn't affected but growth stops and the bulb becomes fibrous.

• Mulch Swiss chard heavily to keep the soil cool and damp, and to keep disease spores from splashing up from the soil onto leaves. A lack of moisture and warm ground make Swiss chard taste bitter.

• Beets grow anywhere, but in cold climates they can be stored in the ground over winter by heaping a 6-inch layer of straw over them to prevent the ground from freezing. Pull up a few to use anytime.

• Beets go dormant, but they retain their small size, tenderness, and sweet flavor. In spring, they will resprout and form seed heads if they have been left in the ground over winter.

Cabbage, Broccoli, Cauliflower, Kohlrabi, and Brussels Sprouts

- Closely space broccoli transplants at planting; crowding promotes more side shoots after the main head is cut.

- Plant kohlrabi seeds directly in the ground after your area's average frost-free date; this vegetable loves cool weather and grows *fast*! Harvest, about 8 weeks after seeding, when the aboveground bulbs are about 2 inches in diameter. If they get much larger, they'll get woody and fibrous. Their cabbagelike leaves are edible.

- Space cabbage transplants at least 18 inches apart in rows for big heads. The cabbage family is notorious for limiting its growth when crowded. Conversely, if small heads are desired, crowd the transplants.

- Wet roots—not heavy rains—make cabbage heads split or rot in the center. Avoid this problem by amending heavy (clay) soils with organic matter or plant in raised beds.

- Brussels sprouts need a long growing period, but they are extremely frost hardy. Direct seed sprouts in your garden four months before your local last frost date.

- When Brussels sprouts begin to form along the stalk, pinch off the tip of the stalk for larger sprouts.

- To avoid cabbage with strong flavor, sidedress with ammonium nitrate, cottonseed meal, or any other high nitrogen fertilizer every 2 weeks.

- For an easy second crop of broccoli, direct seed it between transplants in early spring. About the time the transplants' main heads mature, the seeded plants will be ready to grow to size. Cut off old plants at their base so that new root systems are not disturbed.

- Cut broccoli stems at an angle when you're harvesting them so the stem will shed water to prevent rot.

Carrots

- Seeds take 14 to 21 days to germinate. Soak them overnight in a cup of water and a teaspoon of hydrogen peroxide to speed germination.

- If your soil is clay, build a raised bed for carrots. They need loose soil like loam to form big roots that aren't stunted or misshapen. Also, add bone meal to the growing area a week or two before planting seeds to stimulate the formation of large carrots.

- Place wet cardboard or newspapers over freshly sowed carrot seeds to keep them evenly moist, which is important for germination. Water when the paper dries out so that the soil stays damp.

- Baby carrots are usually ready to harvest in about 45 days. The ones found in grocery stores are actually large carrots that have been pared to "baby" size.

- Plant carrots near legumes to provide extra nitrogen for the carrots. More than other vegetables, carrots can "harvest" the nitrogen affixed to bean, pea, and peanut roots.

- Sunburn is a condition that causes carrots to turn green on their crown, producing a slightly bitter taste. Avoid it by pushing loose soil around developing carrots about 45 days after planting.

- Most carrots are cold hardy and can remain in the ground as long as the soil doesn't freeze. Mulch them thickly with straw or shredded fall leaves to add warmth to the ground and harvest the roots as you need them. In northern climates, cut off the carrot tops, mulch with leaves, add a layer of straw, cover with a plastic sheet, and add a second thick layer of straw.

Corn

- Corn plants have shallow roots and must be watered or irrigated often. Mound soil around the base of small plants to keep them from blowing over in the wind.

- Plant corn in blocks of 16 plants—4 plants wide and 4 plants deep—for optimum pollination. Corn pollen drifts by the wind and will pollinate the closest variety. (But if you save seed, either grow only one variety to insure genetic purity or separate varieties by at least 300 feet.)

- Plant corn at the north side of your garden so the towering stalks don't block sunlight needed by shorter vegetables. Squash and pumpkin vines planted to the south of corn will produce dense crawling vines under the corn plants, which will shade the soil and keep it moist.

- Don't pull off unfertilized ears of corn. Pick them and use as baby corn in Oriental cuisine, salads, or for pickles.

- Raccoons are *the* worst pests in the corn patch. They'll eat half the cob just before its fully ripe or snap it off to take with them. To thwart these bandits, put duct tape about each ear, in the middle of the stalk, and wind the tape down and around to the ear base, circling the stalk.

- Harvest dent or flint corns when their silks are brown and dried. The ears will withstand a couple of light frosts if the silks aren't fully brown. If autumn weather is rainy, harvest and finish drying the ears indoors.

Cucumbers

- Cucumbers are 95 percent water, so cucumber vines need *lots* of water, especially after they've bloomed and set fruits, so keep up the watering. Add extra compost, manure, or other organic fertilizer into the soil to give vines a boost to set more fruit and ripen their crop.

- Mild bitterness is still found in cucumbers due to higher-than-normal levels of cucurbitacin triggered by high temperatures and wide temperature swings. Too little water, as well as uneven watering practices (too wet followed by too dry), low soil fertility, and low soil pH are also stress factors. (Overly mature or improperly stored cucumbers may also develop a mild bitterness, although it is usually not severe enough to prevent gardeners from eating them.)

- Plant nasturtiums, marigolds, sunflowers, or dill near cucumber vines to repel cucumber beetles and numerous other pests. Tall sunflowers make great trellises for the vines too.

- White-skinned varieties start turning yellow as days shorten towards fall, but their flavor is still good. Green-skinned varieties that turn yellow will be bitter, however.

- Harvest early in the morning while cucumbers are full of water, and refrigerate them immediately or pickle them. Chilled cucumbers will last 3 or 4 days in the refrigerator without shriveling and losing flavor. (Grocery store ones have been waxed to keep them hydrated through shipping and distribution.)

Eggplants

- Make sure the soil is full of compost and a small amount of bone meal before planting. Eggplants don't like high levels of nitrogen and needs phosphorous and potassium to flower and fruit.

- Spray plants with Epsom salts dissolved in warm water to stimulate flowering.

- Eggplants won't set fruit if nighttime temperatures are much below 70 degrees F, especially in northern climates. Mulch the plants with aluminum foil to gather the day's heat so that it will radiate back to plants at night. The flowers will set fruit then. Or use floating row covers to trap the day's heat.

- Use Neem oil spray on plant leaves, tops, and bottoms to kill and prevent infestations of whiteflies and spider mites—the two worst eggplant pests.

- The plants and fruits are pretty, so why not display eggplant in containers to set on the deck or patio? Use a 5-gallon pot for each plant, water daily, and apply liquid fertilizer every 2 weeks. In return, the container eggplants will produce an abundant number of glossy, colorful fruits.

- Harvest immature eggplants for the best flavor. If an eggplant loses its glossy look, it's past its prime.

Lettuces

- Plant a row of seeds every 2 weeks from early spring until Labor Day. Refrigerate lettuce seeds for 2 weeks before you sow them in late summer. Seeds need cool ground in which to germinate, but chilling them tricks the seeds into sprouting in warm soil.

- Lettuce demands sweet, fertile soil. Add plenty of slow-release nutrients in the form of compost, composted cow manure, alfalfa pellets, or kelp meal to the ground before planting; add a cup of ground lime or fireplace ashes to every 16 square feet of ground, as lettuce likes high soil pH, between 6.5 to 7.5.

- Don't mulch lettuce beds because the cover provides a welcome home for slugs and earwigs, which will eat outer leaves and destroy the growth center of heading lettuces.

- To thin lettuce seedlings, *cut* them off at the soil level rather than pulling them up. The fragile roots of remaining plants aren't damaged. You can use the cuttings for garnish or eat them in salads.

- If new lettuce leaves develop brown tips, the soil is deficient in calcium. Apply some crushed eggshells to the surrounding soil to quickly remedy the problem.

- Shade lettuce plants in the heat of summer so they don't turn bitter, and keep the lettuce heavily watered.

- Leaves also take light frosts in their stride, extending the season even further. You can push both edges of the growing season by seeding various favorite lettuce varieties in containers. Bring them indoors at night and put back outdoors in direct sun in the morning, even if there is frost on the lawn.

- Lengthen the harvest of late summer-planted lettuces by placing floating row covers over them when the nights turn frosty. Mature lettuce easily survives temperatures into the upper 20s with protection. Newspaper works, too, but sheets need to be removed in the mornings.

Melons

- Watermelon seeds will germinate when the soil is 70 degrees F, while other melon types require 80 degrees F soil temperature for germination. Start those indoors at the same time you direct-seed watermelons and set out plants a couple of weeks later.

- In a cold-climate area with short summers, plant cantaloupes and small specialty melons, such as Tigger, as they will ripen in 90 days or less if you start seeds indoors about three weeks before planting in the ground.

- Melons like alkaline soil with a pH of 6.5 to 7. If your soil is acidic, add lime to the growing bed before planting.

- When melon vines are about 30 inches long, remove the end bud to force branching and increase productivity. More lateral growth results in bigger melons; allow only one or two fruits to form on each vine.

- When vines start to run, spray foliage with a boron mixture (2 tablespoons household borax to 1 gallon warm water). The plants will be stronger and the melons will be sweeter.

- Don't water or irrigate for a week before harvesting melons, even if the vines wilt. Hot, dry weather is what produces high-quality, sweet melons. Rain near harvesting reduces sweetness.

- Encourage ripening by pinching off the fuzzy growth tips of vines. Remove all little fruits 4 or 5 weeks before the end of your area's growing season. The plant's energy will go into ripening the larger melons.

Onions and Garlic

- Start onions from sets or transplants, rather than seed, to shorten their long growing season. When planting sets, space the smallest of them 2 inches apart to harvest as scallions. Bigger sets grow into bigger onions, so space them widely. The opposite applies to onion seedlings. Ones larger than a pencil in diameter do not bulb well and should be grown for scallions.

- Plant garlic cloves in fall when you plant other bulbs such as tulips and daffodils. Each clove will spend the fall and early winter growing a root system.

- There are two types of garlic: hardneck and softneck. The hardneck types send up a stiff flower that produces small cloves. Remove the flower stalk to trigger underground bulb production. Cloves of hardneck types are bigger than softneck varieties. Hardnecks are more cold hardy and perform well in frigid climates. Softnecks are more productive, their bulbs have more cloves, and they store longer than hardneck types. They can be planted in any climate.

- Onions are sensitive to the length of summer days. Ones adapted to the long days (15 to 16 hours) in northern gardens won't bulb and mature in the short days (11 to 12 hours) of the South. Intermediate ones are not daylight sensitive and will grow anywhere. Be sure you select the correct type for your summer day length.

- Dig, don't pull, garlic bulbs when half of the leaves are brown. If you pull, cloves may be left behind. Hang bulbs in a shaded place to cure. Garlic is ready to eat when an outer papery skin develops.

- Grow red onions if you intend to store them. Their pigment is tied to a phenolic acid compound that inhibits rot in onions.

Peas

- Soak pea seeds overnight for quick germination in cool, spring soil. Also, inoculate them with rhizobia powder; peas are legumes that convert nitrogen from the air with the help of that bacterium, which colonizes on pea roots.

- You can't plant peas too early. They'll take freezes, wet ground, and more. Seed them when the ground is workable, within a couple weeks of the last frost date. Plant them in full sunlight, however, because they need a soil temperature of 40 degrees F minimum to germinate.

- In warm climates, mulch peas when seedlings are about 6 inches high with straw or shredded leaves to maintain cool soil temperature while the air temperatures climb.

- For dwarf varieties, use twigs for a trellis; tall varieties do well tied onto chicken wire, strung between stakes.

- Leave some peas on the vine to dry; let them fall to the ground in winter and watch them sprout next spring for a new crop. This lazy-gardener technique works in all but the coldest climates.

- Let soup peas mature and dry on the vine before harvesting. Wash them thoroughly, air dry, and store in sealed containers such as canning jars.

- Split shelling pea pods to harvest tender, sweet green peas for fresh consumption. Any that are left can be frozen or canned for later use. Or, leave the pods and seeds to mature and dry for cooking.

- The entire pod of snap peas, including sweet green peas, is harvested when it's young and tender. Eat them fresh, steam, freeze, or stir-fry for the best flavor.

- Snow peas are picked for their tender, juicy pods—the peas are insignificant. Snow peas are best used fresh or in stir-fry dishes.

Peppers

- Hot peppers love hot ground and air! Hot peppers will be hotter as the temperature rises, so if you want heat and live in the North, buy the hottest varieties available so you won't be disappointed. It's the opposite for the South.

- Peppers don't grow until soil temperature is 65 degrees F or higher, so if cold ground is a problem, put a cage around the transplants and wrap it with plastic to trap the day's heat.

- If heat is a problem with sweet peppers in southern climates, mulch soil thickly to keep it in the optimal temperature range (65 to 75 degrees F) and to retain moisture.

- Throw a teaspoon of soil sulfur in the bottom of each planting hole when setting out transplants. Sulfur acidifies soil slightly, and plants will then use the fertilizer more efficiently.

- After blossoms have set, spray pepper plants with a magnesium solution (1 tablespoon Epsom salts to 1 quart water), or work 1 tablespoon Epsom salts into the ground around each plant. More blossoms will appear and the fruits will be bigger.

- Sweet peppers need a steady supply of water up to harvest. Hot peppers, on the other hand, develop more heat if water is withheld.

- Hot peppers in containers are an excellent way to grow sizzling jalapeños in cooler, northern climates. Set the container on concrete in a full-sun area. Use pots that are at least 3-gallon-sized, so plants grow big and set abundant crops.

Potatoes

- A simple way to produce 35 to 50 pounds of tubers in 16 square feet (a 4-foot by 4-foot bed) is to plant on *top* of the ground. Place whole seed potatoes on top of soil that has been enriched with a 20-pound bag of compost and a cup of balanced organic fertilizer such as kelp meal or alfalfa pellets. Use whole tubers, instead of cutting them into chunks, to avoid rot. After spacing the potatoes about 12 inches apart in every direction, cover the bed with about a foot of straw. *That's all!* You can start harvesting baby or "new" potatoes when the plants flower.

- One-half cup of soil sulfur prevents potatoes from developing scab in alkaline soils. (Ideal pH is 6.0 to 6.5.)

- If potato beetles are a problem in your area, cover young plants with floating row covers to shield them from the insects. Spraying foliage with Bt. (*Bacillus thuringiensis*) will stop beetle eggs from hatching.

- Cut back on watering after potatoes flower. As tubers put on size and mature, too much water causes cracking and rotting.

- To harvest potatoes for storage, wait 2 weeks after plant tops have died before digging them up. During this time, their skins toughen so they don't bruise or tear.

Radishes

- You can broadcast seeds when planting in a row, but thinning is vital. Space developing radishes 4 inches apart for the best-looking and -tasting ones. If they are planted any closer, competition takes over, resulting in small, pithy radishes.

- Plant spring radishes as early as the ground can be worked; they tolerate light freezes and grow rapidly in cool soil. Podding radishes should be sowed after the last freeze, as they produce their pods before the underground radish forms. Winter radishes, which can be stored, should be planted about 2 months before the first frost date for your area. Consult the seed packet for the days-to-maturity and count backwards to get an accurate planting date.

- Radish seeds remain viable for up to 5 years.

- Avoid pests that live in the soil by raising the pH of soil in which you grow radishes by adding fireplace ashes to the seed bed.

- Rat's Tail podding radishes thrive during hot weather, unlike other varieties. Harvest pods during July and August, and then pull up plants. Let some pods dry for seed before removing plants.

- Heavy rains make radish skins crack. Harvest them before the storm; otherwise, wire worms, cabbage root maggots, and other insects will invade, ruining your radishes.

- Small, round varieties, such as Early Scarlet Globe and Sparkler, can be grown in pots indoors during winter. Place the pots in west- or south-facing windows or under grow lights for 10 hours daily.

Squash and Pumpkins

- Plant seeds 3 to 5 weeks after tomatoes go in the ground. Soil must be at least 70 degrees F to direct seed squash and pumpkin.

- Squash and pumpkins are heavy feeders. Prepare the soil by adding generous amounts of compost and composted manure. Sidedress plants with a balanced fertilizer when the blossoms start to set fruits.

- Mulch the planting bed thickly with straw or other organic matter when temperatures rise to keep soil moist. A bonus: the bottoms of developing winter squash and pumpkins won't rot if heavy rains fall.

- Many bush-type squash like Yellow Crookneck can be space hogs. Plant them between caged and staked tomato plants or cage them too. A 4-foot-diameter circle of chicken wire will contain them.

- Squash that produce runners, like Acorn and Delicata, can be trained to a trellis to save space.

- Harvest summer squash 3 to 5 days after flowering for the best quality.

- Winter squash and pumpkins are ready to pick when their stems are drying and their skin has hardened. The best test of this is to try to pierce the skin with your fingernail; if it doesn't pierce, the fruit is ready to harvest.

- Let pumpkins and winter squash "cure" in a warm, dry place for a couple of days before storing. Also, wipe them with a bleach solution (1 tablespoon household bleach to 1 cup water) to kill fungus spores or bacteria that cause rot.

Tomatoes

- Plant the right tomato for your climate. Determinate or bush types produce their entire crop in a few weeks. They are perfect for areas with short seasons. Indeterminate tomatoes, which keep on growing and producing until a killing freeze, do well in hotter climates with long growing seasons. Or plant both: You'll have a large harvest in midsummer from determinates and a smaller, but steady supply of indeterminate tomatoes until frost.

- Don't overfeed plants. Tomatoes produce best with slow-release fertilizers that continually deliver small amounts of nutrients. Fast-release fertilizers result in 10-foot-tall plants and no tomatoes.

- To give plants a boost, especially if they have heavy crops, work some Epsom salts into the soil around the stem or spray a solution on their leaves. Epsom salts are magnesium sulfate, which leaves need to manufacture food.

- Mulch plants thickly with straw, shredded leaves, or any other organic matter. This maintains consistent soil moisture and prevents fungal spores, which spread diseases to plants from splashing up from the soil onto plant foliage.

- Blossom-end rot is caused by inconsistent soil moisture, not lack of calcium in the ground. There is usually plenty of calcium in most soils, but it depends on water to transport it to a plant's roots. So mulch heavily and water at least 1 inch weekly.

- Container-grown tomatoes are easy if you plant them in at least 15 gallons of soil. That's what a 14-inch diameter pot will hold. Even Brandywine and other lanky beefsteak types will thrive. Push a tall cage into the pot when you plant, and water daily.

- Cherry types are especially susceptible to splitting if the soil dries out and is then watered heavily. It's important to keep the soil around all tomatoes evenly moist, but cherries suffer the worst due to their small size.

- Withhold water for 3 to 4 days before harvesting. Tomatoes will be sweeter and more flavorful.

Apples, Pears, and Asian Pears

- Scatter fireplace ashes around the drip line of apple and pear trees in early spring. The ashes supply magnesium, boron, and a host of other elemental nutrients that tree fruits need.

- Go light on the fertilizer with pear trees. They are very thrifty with nitrogen, taking almost all they need from the surrounding soil, even if it is low in nutrients. Pears also "recycle" the nitrogen they take up within the tree. If too much is present, the result is excessive foliage and few or no fruit buds.

- Pick apples when the stem snaps from the tree after you lift up the fruit and let it fall. They are then ready to eat, cook, and store.

- When to pick a pear can be perplexing, because pears do *not* ripen on the tree; they are picked green. Figuring out just when they are in the perfect green state takes practice. Push the pear's surface near its stem with your thumb. If it gives slightly, pick it. Harvest all fruit at this stage and refrigerate them at about 36 degrees F for at least a week. Then bring the pears to room temperature and let them ripen gradually for a couple of days for maximum quality.

- Pick Asian pears when they are fully colored and their stems easily separate from the tree with a small tug.

- Rake up and discard fallen diseased leaves and aborted fruits under trees as soon as they fall. Being a tidy housekeeper goes a long way to preventing diseases and destructive insects from visiting trees again.

Herbs and Edible Flowers

- Plant Mediterranean herbs like thyme, oregano, rosemary, and lavender in gritty soil. Add sand if your soil is compact, and mulch with fine gravel. White turkey grit (found at farm stores) or tiny white pebbles are the best mulch for lavender, as the color reflects light up toward plant leaves so more flowers form.

- Cilantro and dill are cool-season herbs. Plant them early, because summer heat will initiate bolting (going to seed). Plant again in late August.

- Mint, thyme, and tarragon are invasive, so plant them in areas where an attractive, aromatic groundcover is welcome. Or grow in large containers.

- Most herbs don't require extra fertilizer; in fact, excess nitrogen *reduces* the flavor oils in herb leaves. The exceptions are parsley, basil, and dill; they need liquid fertilizer such as fish meal emulsion weekly.

- Keep flowers picked off parsley, as it will try to set seed when temperatures rise. If flowers remain, the plant will put all its energy into forming seed rather than growing more leaves.

- Pinch basil, parsley, and dill regularly to keep plants bushy and discourage flowering.

- Members of the mint family, crosnes are best harvested when the ground heaves around plants in early autumn. Carefully dig them up with your fingers and scrub with a brush to clean the dirt out of all the grooves. The tubers will store in the refrigerator up to 90 days.

How to Start from Seed

Most heirloom vegetables and herbs are available only in seed form. There *are* increasing numbers of garden centers selling heirloom vegetables, fruits, and herb plants, though, due to the building interest in growing heirloom edibles. However, be prepared to plant from seed, because many varieties you will want won't be found at a garden center.

Vegetable and herb seeds such as dill, pumpkins, squash, corn, beans, carrots, and peas can be directly planted in the ground. Others in tuber or bulb form (such as potatoes, onions, and garlic) are also planted directly in the ground. Some, like eggplants, tomatoes, peppers, and basil, need to be planted inside while temperatures outdoors are still cold. The seedlings can grow into sturdy transplants ready to grow rapidly in the garden once you plant them outside. Lettuces, melons, chives, and cabbage (and cabbage relatives like broccoli and cauliflower) can be started either way. Starting seeds as transplants saves valuable time, especially for varieties that have long maturity dates. You can save up to 60 days with cabbage, for instance, if you start seeds indoors three weeks before setting them out in the garden. Warm-weather crops like tomatoes gain 2 months or more.

Starting Transplants

Here's how to get started. First, you'll need a light source. A bright, south-facing window will do, but seedlings will grow better under fluorescent, halogen, or LED plant lights. Supplement window light with a single grow bulb of 1000-watt intensity or a fluorescent light. The most inexpensive light source is a fluorescent 2-tube shop light found at home-improvement and hardware stores. The fixture can be hung on chains from ceiling hooks if you are starting a large number of seeds, or even propped up on bricks on a table. Plenty of plant light racks are available too. No matter what your set-up is, the aim is to position the light source 2 inches above the seed pots and be able to raise the lights so they remain above the tops of seedlings after they sprout. It's important to be able to move the light up and down. Whatever system you choose, put the lights on a timer. Indoor lighting is less intense than sunlight and seedlings require a minimum of 14 hours of light daily; 16 hours is optimum. Once you've assembled your seed-growing apparatus, it's easy to take it down for storage when the transplants go outdoors, and it's simple to reassemble it for the next season.

Seeds sprout best at temperatures that are comfortable for you. Set up your seed-starting equipment in a room at stays at 72 to 75 degrees F during the day and falls no lower than 62 to 65 degrees F at night. Some seeds like basil, tomatoes, and peppers sprout best in very warm soil; a heat mat underneath pots and trays is perfect. Or place the pots on top of the refrigerator, where heat from its coils accumulates, until seeds sprout. Then place the seedlings under lights to grow.

You can start seeds in just about any kind of container. Trays, flats, pots, old egg cartons, cut-off milk cartons, or even take-out food containers are suitable. If the trays or pots have been used before, disinfect them by soaking in a solution of 90 percent water and 10 percent bleach for at least 10 minutes before using. Rinse in clear water after the bleach bath to rinse off any remaining bleach. If you use peat pots, peat seedling strips, or pots made of dried, compressed cow manure, soak them in water before filling with potting mix so they don't rob the mix of water later. Peat can "wick" moisture away from the potting mix.

Fill containers with a commercial seed-starting mix or potting mix. You can make your own mix by combining 4 quarts peat moss and 2 teaspoons ground lime. Don't use garden soil unless it has been sterilized first. Otherwise, weeds, bugs, and diseases will attack seedlings. You can do this at home, though. Sterilize garden soil in the oven by baking it at least 2 hours at 200 degrees F. Wet the potting mix completely before you put it into pots and trays, but pour off any excess water that drains out of container bottoms. Fill the trays and pots to overflowing with mix; then press down until firm. Soil high in a container, where air will flow across it, eliminates damping-off disease, which often plagues seedlings. The tiny seedlings will just fall over and die.

Next, plant the seeds. Some vegetables such as lettuce and parsley germinate better when seeds are scattered on *top* of the planting mix and simply pressed into the soil with your hand. They need the extra light for germination. Sowing instructions on the back of seed packets will specify the correct spacing, planting depth, time to sow, and any other pertinent information for that particular seed variety.

Use *warm* water to moisten seeds for the first 2 or 3 days; they don't like cold showers either. Once seedlings germinate, use water that is at room temperature. Containers should be kept evenly damp but not soaking wet. Too much moisture will cause the seeds to rot. Use a spray bottle to water newly planted seeds and tiny seedlings or, if possible, water from the bottom. If you can, slip your pots and flats into plastic bags to maintain an even humidity and moisture level, and to reduce the frequency of watering. After seeds sprout, add 1 teaspoon of a balanced organic or synthetic liquid fertilizer to a quart of water. Use this weak fertilizer solution once a week to water seedlings until they go into the garden.

After seedlings form two sets of true leaves, they should be thinned or individually potted so there is room for plants to develop naturally. If you thin them, use scissors to cut the stem off at soil level; pulling a seedling out of the mix can damage those that remain. Vegetables that go in the garden while nights are still cold are best thinned. Cabbage, broccoli, and onions are examples. Potting-up seedlings to larger containers is essential for vegetables such as melons, tomatoes, and peppers, which will remain indoors under lights for six weeks or more, waiting for warmer weather. They need room to develop robust root systems and stocky, dark green plants. Adjust lights continually so that they are about 2 to 3 inches above plant tops. Use water-soluble fertilizer once a week. Running a fan next to plants for a couple of hours daily helps them to develop thicker stems. The air motion triggers a hormone that increases cell size.

BUILDING AN EASY INSTANT VEGETABLE GARDEN

Measure a 4-foot by 4-foot square in an area that receives at least 6 hours of direct sunlight daily. Remove any grass or weeds with a hoe. Spread three layers of newspaper over the cleared area. Place landscape timbers, bricks, rocks, or old lumber around the edges to form a border that is at least 4 inches high. Timbers or lumber can be nailed at the corners for added strength. Empty two 40-pound bags of composted cow manure, three 2-cubic-foot bags of topsoil, and one 4-cubic-foot bale of peat moss into the bed. Add 2 cups of fertilizer and 1 cup alfalfa pellets. Mix all the materials together with a hoe or your hands. Water thoroughly before planting. That's it! See, you can do it. Now, let's take a look at those seed catalogs.

A week before planting outdoors, begin to "harden off" transplants. This process acclimates soft and tender plants, which have been protected from cool temperatures and strong sun, to their new environment. Initially, place plants in a shady outdoor area or on an east-facing porch; bring them indoors at night if nighttime temperatures are colder than what plants can tolerate. Each day, move them out into the sun for a few hours, increasing the time spent in direct sunlight each day. Keep them well watered, and don't place them directly on the ground if slugs are a problem. Monitor plants closely for insect damage.

Don't rush to set out plants in the garden. If they won't withstand frost, be sure all danger of frost has passed before setting them out. Water the ground outside and the seedlings thoroughly before transplanting to prevent transplant shock. Try to transplant on a cloudy day or in early evening so that strong sun won't wilt the seedlings. Dig a hole about twice the size of the rootball and set the transplant into the hole so the rootball will be covered by ¼-inch of soil. Press the soil *firmly* around the roots. A small depression around the plant stem will help trap moisture. Top the ground *around* transplants with 1 or 2 inches of organic mulch such as shredded leaves or compost. Water immediately after transplanting and every day for the first week. Be sure to water deeply so plants develop deep root systems.

Tubers and Bulbs

Garlic bulbs and small potato tubers are saved from the previous season to preserve their genetic purity. You can also buy seed potatoes, garlic, and onion sets, which are tiny, mature onions of 1 inch grown from seed. Onions are biennials, requiring two seasons to produce seed. Harvest, dry, and store the best onions from your garden and replant them the following spring. Onions will only sprout after they rest at least 3 months. As the days get longer, each onion forms a seed stalk and flower head, which contains hundreds of tiny flowers. Insects pollinate them, seed is formed, and the plant and flower begin to dry. Seeds are encased in tiny pods that shatter easily. Harvest the pods as soon as they dry. Seeds store up to 2 years. These seeds are used to produce onion sets for the commercial market, and scallions and full-grown onions in the home garden. Start harvesting onions grown from seed about 3 weeks after they sprout green tops. I usually pull every other one for fresh use to space the onions left. They'll have plenty of room to develop large bulbs.

Garlic is grown from the cloves formed in each bulb, the ones you cook. After harvest, dry garlic bulbs by hanging them by their stems for a week or two in an airy, warm place, out of direct sunlight. You can either store them for up to 8 months before planting or plant the cloves in fall. Like onions, garlic needs several months of dormancy before sprouting again. But even in cold climates, fall-planted garlic will stay dormant under mulch until spring and produce bigger bulbs than garlic planted in spring.

When digging up potatoes at the end of summer, reserve the small ones for next year's crop. These tubers are clones of the parent plant and the best way to keep a variety pure. Potato plants will produce flowers and then seed balls, but the seeds contained within do not grow true to the parent. Every seed produces a different variety.

Store seed potatoes in a dark, cold (32 to 40 degrees F) area for up to 6 months. Don't store them near apples, which give off ethylene gas that spurs potato tubers to sprout. A week to ten days before you plant in spring, bring seed potatoes into a warm sunny spot so that their eyes will sprout. You can cut larger potatoes into three or four pieces for planting if each piece has at least two healthy sprouts. Rub the cut surfaces with soil sulfur to prevent fungal diseases like rot and scab. Air dry the pieces at least 24 hours before planting.

Direct Sowing

Many seeds do best when they're sown directly in the ground. Read the seed packets to know when they should be planted (soil temperature), spacing, and planting depth. Seeds are dormant, but you can encourage quick germination by "breaking" their dormancy. Soak them in warm water with a tiny amount of hydrogen peroxide (1 quart water to 1 teaspoon hydrogen peroxide) for 2 hours. Then plant. Legumes such as peas, beans, and peanuts gather nitrogen for growth from the air by using bacteria that attaches to plant roots. Give your plants a head start by wetting the seeds and rolling them in a legume inoculant containing rhizobia bacteria, which can be found in seed catalogs and at garden centers. Plants will be hardier and produce bigger crops, plus their roots will deposit excess nitrogen in the soil for other plants to use. Other seeds benefit from being inoculated with mycorrhizal fungi. It colonizes on plant roots, from the first hair roots to large taproots, and mines the soil for nutrients and water. Legumes don't benefit from the fungi. Mycorrhizae inoculants can be found in seed catalogs and at garden centers specializing in organic gardening. Use mycorrhizae on transplants too. Rub a small amount of the inoculants over plant roots just before you plant.

Quick Soil Primer

Healthy seedlings, tubers, bulbs, and transplants won't grow well unless the garden soil in which they are planted is fertile and ready to support vigorous growth. Add slow-release nutrients to established garden beds by spreading a 2-inch layer of compost or composted cow manure over the top of the ground. Then sprinkle a cup or two of slow-release fertilizer or rabbit food over every 16 square feet of planting bed. Rabbit food is basically compressed alfalfa meal pellets, which are nitrogen- and phosphorus-rich. Alfalfa also contains large quantities of a hormone called triacontanol, which stimulates cell division and growth in all plants. You can buy rabbit food or alfalfa pellets at pet and farm feed stores.

After layering the nutrients, water your planting beds deeply; water newly sown seeds and transplants daily for the first week. After seedlings are 1 or 2 inches high and you've thinned them, mulch the entire bed, even between seedlings. Two to four inches of incomplete compost, shredded leaves or fine bark make good mulch. Grass clippings are good if the lawn from which they came has not been treated with weed killer. These chemicals persist and will kill seedlings. Also, clippings tend to clump and mat, especially when they're wet, spawning diseases. Mix grass clippings with leaves or bark to prevent this.

Saving Your Own Seeds

By growing heirloom edibles, you've become part of the endless process of saving seeds for the next generation. "All farmers and gardeners have saved their own seeds for most of the last 10,000 years, the span of modern agriculture," says Bill McDorman, president of Seeds Trust in Cornville, Arizona. He's one of the most authoritative sources on how to save seeds and has been teaching classes on the topic for over 30 years. "The ritual of seed saving, in every corner of the world, created the rich agricultural heritage we inherited. Only since the 1930s have the majority of American gardeners and farmers become seed consumers instead of seed savers," McDorman explains. "Since then, up to 80 percent of agricultural genetic diversity has been lost. By saving seeds in their own gardens, home gardeners rejoin this important ritual, taking the genetics of plants from this year into the next one. Fortunately, this is easy. It's the way gardening has always been done." Be a part of the unbroken chain of antiquity and save seeds from a few of your favorite plants this year. Share with other gardeners and pass along the history, taste and appearance of heirlooms you've savored and treasured. McDoman offers free detailed instructions on his Seeds Trust website—go to: www.seedsave.org. Some of the information here came from that site.

Techniques

Separation: Space plants widely, far enough apart from others in the same botanical family so that cross-pollination doesn't take place.

Caging: When plant flowers spread their pollen indiscriminately by wind or insects, cage the plant from which seed will be saved and hand-pollinate flowers. A wire cage covered with floating row cover or fine mesh will do the job inexpensively. After small fruits form, the cover or cage can be removed.

Root to Seed: Biennials such as broccoli and carrots don't produce seed until their second season in the ground. Dig up the plants, including their roots, and store them in a cold, dark area during winter. Make sure plant roots stay hydrated; mist them every week or two. Set plants back in the garden when soil thaws. They will produce flower stalks, flowers, and seed within a couple of months. Carrots can be overwintered in the ground in most climates by cutting off their foliage, burying them under 12 inches of shredded leaves, and covering the bed with a tarp for extra insulation.

Seed Harvesting Methods

Fermentation: Seeds that are encased in a slimy "gel," such as tomatoes and cucumbers, are harvested this way. Squeeze or scoop the gel that contains seeds into a large paper cup or glass jar. Add a little water to hydrate the gel. Cover the jar loosely and place it in a warm area for 3 days; stir daily. As the mixture starts to ferment, you'll know by the putrid smell and white scum that grows on top of the liquid. This fungal mass eats away the gel encasing the seeds and produces an antibiotic that prevents the passage of seed-borne diseases. Pull off this fungal film, add warm water to the fermented seeds, pour everything through a fine mesh strainer, and rinse seeds 3 to 4 times. Remove any skin or flesh particles and spread the seeds on paper plates to dry. Gently separate any clumps of dried seeds.

Flail: Crush or fracture seedpods to free seeds such as peas and broccoli. Rub smaller, thin-skinned pods between your fingers and walk over pea pods dried on the vine to open their tough pods. Then, winnow (separate) the pods to gather clean seeds.

Winnow: Place small seeds and accompanying bits of dried debris on a solid surface. Blow air over the surface so that the lighter chaff flies away and heavier seeds remain. Larger seeds can be cleaned in a similar manner, but it will take a stronger blast of air for dried pods to fly away.

How to Process Seeds

Easy Vegetables for New Seed Savers

Bean: Grow different varieties 150 feet apart so that cross-pollination doesn't occur, or grow just one variety. Wait until the pods are brown and completely dry before harvesting. If you are saving a small amount of seed, open the pods by hand and pull out the dried seeds. Flail larger amounts; crushing them with your feet is a fast way to open the pods. Then pick off large chaff by hand and winnow (separate) the fine remainders.

Lettuce: Space varieties at least 20 feet apart to maintain seed purity. Wait 3 weeks after seed heads flower to harvest. Cut off the top half of the plant, placing it (including the seed head) upside-down in a paper bag to dry further. Shake the bags daily to release mature seeds. After a week or so, rub your hands over seed heads to free the remaining seeds. It may be necessary to winnow seeds to remove any chaff.

Peas: Plant different varieties at least 50 feet apart, or stagger plantings so that each variety blooms at a different time. Let the pods turn brown and dry, about a month after the eating stage. Like beans, hand-harvest seeds from pods if you're saving small amounts. Flail and winnow large amounts.

Tomato: Heirloom varieties have long anthers in the middle of their flowers, which trap pollen from any tomato within 150 to 250 feet. Either plant only one variety or cage plants before they bloom. If you cage them, use a small watercolor brush to spread pollen from flower to flower on the plants. Be sure to fully swipe the anthers for good pollination. Tomato flowers are self-fertile, but the brush technique ensures that each one gets pollinated. Wait until tomatoes are fully ripe before harvesting seeds. (Use the fermentation method detailed under "Seed Harvesting Methods".)

Intermediate Vegetables for Experienced Gardeners

Corn: Separation between varieties is critical, because pollen can blow almost a mile and corn is wind-pollinated. Usually, 1,000 feet between different varieties is reasonable, but some impurity will occur. Save the seeds from at least half of your seed corn plants to avoid intense inbreeding, a condition that results in stunted plants, small ears, and lack of flavor. Harvest seed about 6 weeks after the eating stage. If your growing season is short, pick ears after the husks turn brown and store them in a cool, dry place. Pull back the husks so that kernels continue to dry. Grasp dry ears in your hands and twist your hands around the cob; the kernels will fall into a container placed below.

Cucumber: Because pollen can travel over a half-mile, plant only one variety or hand-pollinate several. Save seeds from at least 6 cucumbers to get the best seed purity and genetic strength. Choose overripe fruits, ones that are at least 6 weeks beyond the eating stage and that are gold colored. Slice the cucumber lengthwise, scoop out its seeds, and place in a large jar. Follow the instructions for fermentation to prepare the seeds.

Melons: Separate melons by a half-mile to prevent cross-pollination or hand-pollinate, which is difficult due to the small size of their flowers. One watermelon and one melon variety can be planted next to each other because they are from two different plant families and don't cross. Harvest seeds from ripe melons that were picked to eat; scoop out melon seeds and pick out watermelon seeds. Rinse them until they're clean and spread over paper plates or towels to dry.

Radish: Multiple varieties must be separated by at least a half-mile to ensure seed purity. Radishes (except podding radishes) are biennials and produce their seeds in their second season. Use the root-to-seed technique detailed previously, replanting at 9-inch intervals. Harvest the 3-foot-tall seed stalks when the pods turn brown and are dry. Flail and winnow to prepare seeds for storage.

Squash and Pumpkin: Squash of different categories can be planted together, but those in the same group like Yellow Crookneck and Zucchini, as well as pumpkins, need at least a half-mile of isolation for pure seeds. Harvest fully ripe fruits with hard rinds. (Leave summer squash on the vine for an extra 3 to 4 weeks so that their tender skin hardens into rind.) After harvesting, let all squash and pumpkins sit for another month. Then cut open the fruits, scoop out seeds, and rinse them in a wire strainer with warm water until the seeds are clean. Dry the seeds on paper plates or towels.

Advanced Vegetables for Experts

Beet and Swiss Chard: Grow only one variety at a time because both cross readily. Use the root-to-seed method, harvesting plants in fall. Replant early in spring with the plant tops barely above the soil line. Cut the mature foliage loaded with seeds just above plant tops. Let them dry another 2 or 3 weeks. Then strip the seeds from the stalks by hand. For large amounts, pound on bagged stalks to release seeds; then winnow.

Cabbage, Broccoli, Cauliflower, and Brussels Sprouts: All vegetables and varieties in the Brassica family cross-pollinate readily and must be separated by at least 1,000 feet. Caging and hand-pollination works well. Use the root-to-seed method to produce seeds. Dig up the entire plant in fall, trim its leaves, and store it a cold, humid, dark basement to trigger dormancy. Replant in early spring and hand-harvest seedpods when they turn brown and crisp. Crush pods with a hammer and winnow to clean.

Carrot: Because Queen Anne's lace, the wildflower cousin of the carrot, is so prevalent it's difficult to insure seed purity without caging plants. Use the root-to-seed method to produce seed, making sure you include this step: Leave carrots in the ground, but cut off the green foliage when it starts to turn brown in fall. Mulch heavily with shredded leaves, and top with a tarp or blankets. The insulation keeps the ground from freezing, and the carrots go into dormancy. In spring, when green tops appear, remove the mulch and pick the carrots you want to cage for seed saving. When immature flowers appear on the carrot plants, cage and pollinate the blooms with a paintbrush. Hand-pick the seed umbels when they turn brown and winnow the seeds.

Onion: Plant only one type of onion, bunching onion or garlic, as all in the onion family cross readily with others within their species. Separation of one mile is needed or cage plants to insure genetic purity. Use the root-to-seed method, replanting in early spring. Chilling or vernalization (a long exposure to cold such as after winter) is needed to induce flowering; refrigerate the stored onion or garlic bulbs for two weeks before planting. Harvest by cutting off the seed heads when most of the flowers are dry. Store them in a cool, dry area for an additional 2 weeks. Then strip the seed heads with your fingers to free the seeds.

Storage Methods

Long-term storage of what you grow depends on what you want to do with it. For example, do you prefer potatoes that you can use a year from now? If yes, then fresh or dried are the best options. Or do you prefer a quick, already cooked addition to a meal? In that case, canned or frozen would be your best options. Pick the methods that suit your needs when preserving and storing heirlooms you grow or buy at farmers' markets.

Fresh Storage

- **Apple:** Store apples in a root cellar or dark, cool basement or garage. Isolate them, because the ethylene gas they give off makes many vegetables sprout and rot. Most varieties store 3 to 6 months.

- **Asian Pear:** Store Asian pears in sealed bags in the refrigerator to keep them from dehydrating. Use within 60 days.

- **Beet:** Cut beet tops off and store beets in a root cellar or cool, dark area in a single layer on dry sand or cat litter. Use within 2 months.

- **Cabbage, Cauliflower, Broccoli, and Brussels Sprouts:** Harvest mature heads, roots and all. Hang them upside down in a humid basement, garage, or outbuilding where the temperature doesn't drop below freezing. They will keep up to a month.

- **Carrot:** Leave carrots in the ground in the garden. Cut off any green foliage; cover carrots with a foot or more of shredded leaves or straw. Top with a tarp to keep soil from freezing. Harvest as needed.

- **Garlic:** Harvest garlic and let it dry for a week in a sunny location. Then hang bulbs in open mesh bags in a dry, airy place or braid dried plants together.

- **Onion:** Store onions in mesh bags or open baskets in a cool, dry place.

- **Potato:** Store potatoes in a cool, dark place in paper bags with holes poked in them for ventilation. Don't store potatoes near onions, which give off ethylene gas, causing potatoes to sprout. Do not expose to light, which also triggers sprouting, and don't store in the refrigerator; cold destroys their flavor. Potatoes will keep up to 2 months.

- **Winter Squash and Pumpkin:** Clean the squash and pumpkins with bleach and water to kill any fungi or bacteria on the rind. Store in a cool spot up to 6 months.

(Note: Cool temperatures are from 50 to 60 degrees F.)

Root Cellars

Old-fashioned root cellars where gardeners stored vegetables over the winter have virtually disappeared from modern homes. Instead of dirt-floor cellars, basements today have concrete floors and are partially heated by furnaces operating there. But you can build a quick version of an old-time root cellar in less than an hour.

Before the ground freezes for winter, dig a large, deep hole in a sheltered spot, preferably close to the house. Sink a 32-gallon heavy-duty plastic trash can into the hole, positioning it so the rim is about 3 inches above the soil line. That way melting snow and rain will not leak inside. Line the bottom of the trashcan with a 2-inch layer of damp sand, add a layer of vegetables, top with an inch of damp sand and another layer of carrots, potatoes, or whatever you are storing. Repeat the layers, ending up with sand on top. Place the lid on it and top with a 2-foot-high mound of straw or shredded leaves. A sheet of white plastic film over the top will keep everything in place and dry. Anchor the plastic with rocks or bricks.

Freezing

If you have plenty of freezer space, this method preserves vegetables and herbs almost as fresh and nutritionally equal to ones straight out of the garden. Blanch vegetables in boiling water and immediately dunk them into ice water or steam and ice them before freezing. This stops the ripening process and ensures that frozen vegetable will be firm and full of flavor. Package blanched vegetables in heavy-duty plastic bags or plastic cartons designed for freezing. Vegetables can be stored up to a year if the packages are sealed completely.

Broccoli and Cauliflower: Remove the leaves and woody ends of broccoli and cauliflower or cut into florets. Blanch 3 minutes or steam 5 minutes.

Brussels Sprouts: Remove Brussels sprouts from their stalks and sort for size. Blanch small ones 2 minutes, medium ones 4 minutes, and large ones 5 minutes. Steaming isn't recommended.

Carrot: Wash and scrape carrots, then dice or slice them. Blanch or steam 2 minutes.

Corn: Blanch or steam small ears 7 minutes; medium ears 9 minutes; and large ears 11 minutes. For whole kernel corn, blanch on the cob 5 minutes, then dunk the ears in ice water and cut the kernels off the cob.

Green Bean: Remove the ends and strings from green beans if necessary. Blanch 4 minutes or steam 3 minutes.

Herbs: Wash and dry herbs on paper towels. Seal in a plastic bag or glass jar.

Peas: Green peas should be blanched 1 to 1 ½ minutes. Remove the strings from Sugar Snap and Snow peas, and blanch 3 minutes or steam 2 minutes.

Hot Pepper: Wash, dry, and freeze hot peppers in plastic bags or jars.

Summer Squash: Cut summer squash into pieces and blanch 3 minutes or steam 2 minutes.

Drying

Dehydrating: Most fruits, vegetables, and herbs can be dehydrated for storage. Use an electric dehydrator for the best results. It uses far less energy than a gas or electric oven and provides a consistent drying temperature, which is difficult for an oven to do at temperatures lower than 200 degrees F. And there are other factors to recommend drying; Asian pear slices, for instance, maintain their nutritional values and gain concentrated flavor when they're dehydrated. Dried cherry tomatoes are wonderful in salads, bruschetta, and pasta.

Air Drying: Herbs work best with air drying. Tie herb stalks together and hang them to dry in a warm place out of the sun. Or, place two handfuls of herbs, picked late morning when the leaves are dry, in a paper grocery bag. Close the bag with a clip or clothespin and place it in your car trunk. Every day or two, shake the sack to see if leaves are dry and crisp. When the leaves are completely dried, store them in a glass jar in a dark spot such as a pantry or kitchen cabinet.

Canning

The initial investment in a pressure canner, jars, and lids may be a bit costly, but you only buy them once (except the lids). For some foods, you do not need to pressure can. Details on how to can specific foods are lengthy but the basic instructions come with canning jars and the canner. Canning books are inexpensive, too; check out Daniel Gasteiger's book *Yes, You Can! And Freeze and Dry It, Too* (Cool Springs Press, 2010). Visit www.coolspringspress.com to order it. Jars of canned food are safe to eat for several years if the jar's seal remains intact. Store in a dark place such as cupboards, a pantry, or the basement so that light doesn't degrade the food's quality.

Seed and Farmers' Markets Resources

Although you can tell what some of these sites provide by their names, I am purposely not explaining them in detail because it's so much fun to investigate them. Who knows the fascinating heirlooms you'll discover on your own?

If you want to locate local farmers' markets, try this site: Local Harvest, at www.localharvest.org, for a state-by-state listing.

Sources for Seeds

Abundant Life Seed Foundation
(541) 767-9606
www.abundantlifeseeds.com

Baker Creek Heirloom Seeds
(417) 924-8917
www.rareseeds.com

Botanical Interests
(720) 880-7293
www.botanicalinterests.com

Bountiful Gardens
(707) 459-6410
www.bountifulgardens.org

Cherry Gal
(888) 752-0022
www.cherrygal.com

Fedco Seeds
(207) 873-7333
www.fedcoseeds.com

Goodwin Creek Gardens
(800) 846-7359
www.goodwincreekgardens.com

D. Landreth Seed Co.
(800) 654-2407
www.landrethseeds.com

J. L. Hudson, Seedsman
Internet Only
www.jlhudsonseeds.net

Johnny's Selected Seeds
(877) 564-6697
www.johnnyseeds.com

Nichols Garden Nursery
(800) 422-3985
www.nicholsgardennursery.com

Pinetree Garden Seeds
(207) 926-3400
www.superseeds.com

Ronnigers
(800) 314-1955
www.potatogarden.com

Seed Savers Exchange
(563) 382-5990
www.seedsavers.org

Seeds of Change
(888) 762-7333
www.seedsofchange.com

Seeds Trust
(928) 649-3315
www.seedstrust.com

Southern Exposure Seed Exchange
(540) 894-9480
www.southernexposure.com

Territorial Seed Co.
(800) 626-0866
www.territorialseed.com

Tomato Growers Supply
(888) 478-7333
www.tomatogrowers.com

Totally Tomatoes
(800) 345-5977
www.totallytomatoes.com

Wood Prairie Farm
(800) 829-9765
www.woodprairie.com

Sources of Fruit Trees and Plants

Bay Laurel Nursery
(805) 466-3406
www.baylaurelnursery.com

Maple Valley Orchards & Nursery
(920) 842-2904
www.maplevalleyorchards.com

Raintree Nursery
(800) 391-8892
www.raintreenursery.com

St. Lawrence Nurseries
(315) 265-6739
www.sln.potsdam.ny.us/

Trees of Antiquity
(805) 467-9909
www.treesofantiquity.com

Feeding the Hungry

Plant a Row for the Hungry
(877) 492-2727
www.gardenwriters/org.par

Feeding America

(800) 771-2303
www.feedingamerica.org

Seed Saving Exchanges

Landis Valley Museum Heirloom Seed Project
(717) 569-0401
www.landisvalleymuseum.org/

Landis Valley Museum is home to the Heirloom Seed Project. Established in the mid-1980s, the Heirloom Seed Project's focus is on seed preservation and seeds from heirloom varieties of vegetables, herbs, and ornamentals that have historical significance for Pennsylvania Germans from 1750 to 1940.

Native Seeds/SEARCH
(520) 622-5561
www.nativeseeds.org

Native Seeds/SEARCH is a non-profit organization that conserves, distributes, and documents the adapted and diverse varieties of agricultural seeds, their wild relatives, and the roles these seeds play in cultures of the American Southwest and Northwest Mexico.

Organic Seed Alliance
(360) 385-7192
www.seedalliance.org

Organic Seed Alliance is an online seed-saving and species development information site. It is a nonprofit public charity that supports the ethical development and steward-ship of the genetic resources of agricultural seed.

Seed Savers Exchange
(563) 382-5990
www.seedsavers.org

Seed Savers Exchange is the largest seed-saving organization in the United States. It maintains over 24,000 heirloom varieties on its 890-acre Heritage Farm.

The Thomas Jefferson Center for Historic Plants
(800) 243-0743
www.monticello.org/chp

The Thomas Jefferson Center for Historic Plants, established at Monticello in 1987, collects and distributes historic plant varieties. The program centers on Thomas Jefferson's horticultural interests and the plants he grew at Monticello, but covers the broad history of plants cultivated in America by including varieties documented through the nineteenth century and choice North American plants, a group of special interest to Jefferson himself.

Bibliography

Ashworth, Suzanne. *Seed to Seed*. Seed Savers Publications, 1991.

Ausubel, Kenny. *Seeds of Change*. Harper Collins, New York, 1994.

Bader, Dr. Myles H. *6,001 Food Facts and Chef's Secrets*. Mylin Publishing, 1995.

Crockett, James. *Vegetables and Fruits*. Henry Holt & Company, New York, 1972.

Eames-Sheavly, Marcia and Farrell, Tracy. *The Humble Potato*. Cornell University, Ithaca, New York, 1995.

Hansen, Beth, Editor. *Buried Treasures, Tasty Tubers of the World*. Brooklyn Botanic Gardens, Inc., New York, 2007.

Male, Carolyn. *100 Heirloom Tomatoes for the American Garden*. Workman Publishing, New York, 1999.

Morgan, Joan & Richards, Alison. *The Book of Apples*. Brogdale Horticultural Trust, 1993.

National Research Council. *Lost Crops of the Incas*, Report of an Ad Hoc Panel of the Advisory Committee on Technology Innovation Board on Science and Technology for International Development. National Academy Press, Washington D.C., 1989.

Parsons, Jerry. *Onion Laws*. Texas A&M University, College Station, Texas, http://aggie-horticulture.tamu.edu/plantsanswers/publications/onions/onionlaws.html

Patent, Greg & Patent, Dorothy Hinshaw. *A Is for Apple*. Broadway Books, New York, 1999.

Pollan, Michael. *The Omnivore's Dilemma*. Penguin Books, New York, 2006.

Rupp, Rebecca. *Blue Corn & Square Tomatoes*. Storey Communications, Inc., North Adams, MA, 1987.

Staub, Jack. *75 Exciting Vegetables for Your Garden*. Gibbs Smith, Layton, Utah, 2005.

Stilphen, George Albert. *The Apples of Maine*. Stilphen Crooked River Farms, 2000.

Strickland, Sue with Kent Whealy. *Heirloom Vegetables, A Home Gardener's Guide to Finding and Growing Vegetables from the Past*. Fireside, 1998.

Tuxill, John. *The Biodiversity that People Made*. WORLD WATCH (Worldwatch Institute), May/June 2000.

Vilmorin-Andrieux, M.M. *The Vegetable Garden*. Ten Speed Press, Berkeley, California, reprint of 1885 English edition.

Watson, Benjamin. *Taylor's Guide to Heirloom Vegetables*. Houghton Mifflin Company, New York, 1996.

Weaver, William Woys. *100 Vegetables and Where They Came From*. Algonquin Books, Ashville, North Carolina, 2000.

Weaver, William Woys. *Heirloom Vegetable Gardening*. Henry Holt and Company, New York, 1997.

In My Own Words

Jim Long

In the early days of my herb business (Long Creek Herbs), I was struggling with ways to market them. I grow around 100 varieties of culinary herbs and I thought it might be profitable to explore selling to the chefs of upscale restaurants in my area. I inquired at several restaurants and soon learned that most conventional chefs had never used fresh herbs. One told me that he had no real idea what fresh dill or rosemary even looked like. Since I live in a tourist area I discovered that tourist restaurants aren't as interested in quality as they are quantity of food. I asked the chef of the once-famous Dairy Hollow House Restaurant in Eureka Springs, Arkansas, if he would be interested in buying my herbs and was met with an enthusiastic "yes." The chef drove to my farm one week to get his fresh herb order; the alternating week I delivered his order.

Most fresh herbs from suppliers are bought by the pound, and during the first few weeks, that was what I furnished. But the restaurant was a small, exclusive boutique establishment and the chef said they were throwing a lot of herbs away each week. I hit upon the idea of selling my herbs by the dozen instead of the pound. I bundled each variety into a dozen 6- to 10-inch sprigs, and the chef would order 5 or 8 bundles of each herb he wanted. The profit was actually better for me than when I was selling by the pound, and the chef was pleased because it cut down on waste. I furnished the restaurant with edible flowers, baby heirloom vegetables, and fresh herbs. When *Gourmet* magazine editors came to do a story on the restaurant, they also contacted me as the organic supplier and featured my farm as well.

The experiment was a good one, and what I learned from two seasons of selling fresh-cut herbs was that it would be profitable if the restaurants were close (my average customer was 30 miles away), and if there were a dozen restaurants to supply. Because of those factors I turned my attention to dried herb products and only occasionally filled special fresh-cut orders from chefs.

In My Own Words

Mayo Underwood

I learned about gardening and saving seeds from my Native American (Mohawk) uncle during many summers spent in Maine, beginning when I was five. It never occurred to me that what he taught me I'd use in a business. As I was recovering from a motorcycle accident in which I broke my neck in 1993, my daughter Maren taught me how to use her computer. She suggested that I catalog all the seeds I had collected for years from all over the world. Wherever we lived, I grew, saved, and swapped vegetable, herb, and flower seeds. That initial list became Underwood Gardens seed catalog. We mailed it to about 300 people initially—friends, relatives, gardeners I knew, and the heads of Garden Clubs of America and Illinois. When I sold the company in 2007, more than 70,000 catalogs were being mailed.

The real story is about the many passionate gardeners who gave us seeds to propagate, seeds they had in their families for generations. We had a booth at the Chicago Flower Show in the mid-1990s, and a man stopped to say he had a great tomato, and he'd send seeds. He didn't give me any contact information, but about five years later, he did send a few seeds. They came from Mr. Mong, his elderly father's even older neighbor in Iowa. The three plants that grew produced bright red, dessert-plate-sized fruits with succulent flavor. The Mong tomato was voted Best Tomato of the Year by *Organic Gardening* magazine in 2004.

Underwood Gardens got seeds for *Melothria scabra* from a Southern customer, and we grew the tiny fruit that looked like mini watermelons and tasted like sour cucumbers. We introduced them into the market as Cucamelon in the late 1990s. The tiny delights were grown for centuries throughout Mexico. By that time, larger seed companies were ordering odd heirlooms from us and they were growing them in much larger quantities than we could. They would rename the varieties and introduce them as their exclusives. This particular melon is now commonly available as Mexican Sour Gherkin.

In My Own Words

Deborah Phillips

It is not hard to understand my love of heirloom varieties. My mother's family came from Turin, Italy, in the Piedmont. My grandfather had a restaurant until his too-early death and my great Zio and Zia were vintners until their deaths a few decades ago. My grandmother fed a family of eight during the Depression from a garden the size of most driveways today. I have vivid sensory memories of her unique spaghetti sauce (sugo) and ravioli, which were legendary in her large extended family. Grandma also canned much of what she grew, her earthen cellar crammed with jars. Dinner at Grandma's took hours, and was composed of many courses, with many relatives squeezed around a large dining table in a very small dining room.

Both my parents gardened, though their motivations differed from Grandma's. My mother had large beds of hundreds of exquisite flowers, and they provided ample cuttings for her vases. My father, on the other hand, took pride in the landscaping, rich with spring flowering shrubs and a large walnut tree. But his real passion was fruit. He grew Concord table grapes, raspberries, and strawberries. He won ribbons at the local county fair for his jam. Garden beds were enriched every fall with manure from the neighboring dairy farm.

When I left the nest for the big city, I was frustrated for a few years by not having my own piece of earth to tend. When my husband and I finally moved to a small house with a 15 x 20-foot space in the back, which took four people, a pickax, and tons of soil amendments to make viable, I happily put in small beds of tomatoes, rhubarb, and beans. A few years later, when I relocated to a neighborhood that offered a community garden, I enthusiastically signed up, snagging one of the better plots by sheer good timing. It was a great period of learning for me, not only my own experiments and discoveries, but also the wisdom of the older, more experienced gardeners was invaluable. I still rely on much of it today. They came from all parts of the country, with mixed ethnic heritages, so I spent many hours resting at the picnic table in the shade of the great oak tree there, enjoying the fellowship of my gardening neighbors and comparing notes (and recipes) on heritage varieties.

Two books channeled my early gardening interest: *Culpeper's Herbal*, an ancient compendium of herbal medicine, and Euell Gibbon's *Stalking the Wild Asparagus*. I feel truly blessed that ultimately heirloom gardening provided a livelihood. Growing heirlooms provides an inexhaustible supply of discovery. Whether it is learning how to grow mushrooms, exploring Ayurvedic medicinals, or reading about Peruvian potatoes or Native American varietal history, I am never without an opportunity to learn. It is intensely satisfying and it keeps me young. It also indulges my love of history and need for a sense of connectedness in these turbulent modern times.

Recently, my son sent me pictures of his Brooklyn, New York, apartment garden— gorgeous vegetables from small raised beds in a postage stamp garden. I was proud that my lifelong passion had passed to the next generation. And, with the birth of my granddaughter, the promise of yet another.

Photography Credits

Cool Springs Press would like to thank the following contributors to *Heirloom Flavor, Yesterday's Best-Tasting Vegetables, Fruits, and Herbs for Today's Cook.*

Ed Rode Photography: Front cover and title page

Valerie Garner/Alamy: Page 197 (right)
John Glover/Alamy: Page 196
Mira/Alamy: Pages 164 (top), 227
Stuwdamdorp/Alamy: Page 193
Rob Walls/Alamy: Page 197 (left)
WILDLIFE GmbH/Alamy: Page 121 (bottom)

Annie's Heirloom Seed: Page 126

Baker Creek: Pages 27 (bottom), 29 (all), 36 (bottom), 45, 46 (all), 50 (top), 89 (bottom), 110, 111 (bottom), 150, 154, 181 (bottom), 206 (top), 209 (right), 210 (right), 211 (top right)

Cathy Barash: Page 211 (top left)

Courtesy Bill Bird: Page 108 (bottom)

David Cavagnaro: Pages 26 (top right), 27 (top left), 27 (top left and right), 31, 37 (all), 38, 39, 49 (left), 51, 56 (all), 57 (top), 64 (left), 66 (top), 68(right), 74 (top), 77 (top), 80, 82, 83, 95 (top left and bottom), 97 (top), 98 (all), 99, 100 (all), 101, 106 (top and bottom right), 107 (top), 108 (top), 116 (bottom), 118 (top), 119 (top), 134 (bottom and top right), 135(bottom right), 136 (left), 137 (top and right), 142 (all), 143 (left), 144 (bottom), 145 (top), 152, 153, 155, 160 (bottom), 161 (bottom), 162 (left), 162 (top and bottom right), 165 (top), 171 (all), 172 (bottom), 173 (bottom), 174 (all), 175 (all), 176, 178, 179 (top), 181 (top), 191 (bottom), 194 (top), 206 (bottom), 207 (top left and bottom), 208 (top right), 216 (all), 223, 228 (bottom left), 240 (top left)

CPi: page 233

Dwight Smith/Dreamstime.com: Page 161 (top)

Tom Eltzroth: Pages 95 (top right), 119 (bottom), 127 (bottom), 207 (right), 208 (top left and bottom), 209 (left)

Copyright © Doreen G. Howard: Pages 36 (top), 64 (right), 69, 74 (bottom), 75 (all), 76 (left and top), 77 (bottom), 78 (all), 79 (all), 81, 89 (top), 94 (right), 96, 107 (bottom), 111 (top), 130, 135 (bottom left), 136 (top right), 143 (right), 144 (top), 172 (top), 173 (top), 177 (all), 180, 188, 189, 190 (all), 191 (top), 194 (middle), 195 (all), 199 (all), 210 (left), 211 (bottom), 217, 228 (right)

Imagebroker.net/Photography: Page 120 (bottom)

iStockphoto.com: Pages 10, 44 (all), 47, 49 (right), 116 (top), 151 (top), 218

Native Seed Search: Pages 109 (top), 118 (bottom), 136 (bottom right)

Courtesy Seed Savers Exchange: Page 16 (website)

Comstock/Thinkstock: Page 22
Hemera/Thinkstock: Pages 40, 48 (top), 65 (top right), 88 (top), 138, 156, 202
iStockphoto/Thinkstock: Pages 4 (all), 5 (all), 6, 13, 14, 20-21, 27 (upper right), 30 (left), 32, 48 (bottom), 52, 57 (bottom), 66 (bottom), 70, 84, 102, 166, 182-183, 184, 200-201
Valueline/Thinkstock: Page 146

Shutterstock.com: Pages 18, 24 (bottom), 26 (upper left), 34 (bottom), 42 (bottom), 54 (bottom), 60, 62 (bottom), 72 (bottom), 86 (bottom), 92 (bottom), 104 (bottom), 112, 114 (middle and bottom), 122, 124 (bottom), 132 (bottom), 134 (top left), 140 (bottom), 148 (bottom), 158 (middle and bottom), 164 (bottom), 168 (bottom three), 186 (middle and bottom), 192 (top), 194 (bottom), 204 (bottom four), 212-213, 214, 230, 236, 240 (right), 243 (all)

Courtesy Jane Sperr: Page 76 (bottom right)

Stockbyte/Getty Images: Pages 24 (top), 34 (top), 42 (top), 54 (top), 62 (top), 72 (top), 86 (top), 90, 92 (top), 104 (top), 114 (top), 124 (top), 132 (top), 140 (top), 148 (top), 158 (top), 168 (top), 186 (top), 204 (top)

Susan Thomas, FarmgirlFare.com: Page 58

Claire Davies/Gap Photo/Visuals Unlimited, Inc.: Page 179 (bottom)
Wally Eberhardt/Visuals Unlimited, Inc.: Page 127 (top)
Ken Lucas/Visuals Unlimited, Inc.: Pages 117 (top right), 145 (bottom)
S&O/Gap Photo/Visuals Unlimited, Inc.: Page 192 (bottom)
David Sieren/Visuals Unlimited, Inc.: Page 135 (top)

Scott Vlaun: Pages 26 (bottom), 28 (bottom), 30 (right), 50 (bottom), 59, 65 (top left), 67, 68 (left), 88 (bottom), 94 (left), 97 (bottom), 106 (left), 109 (bottom), 117 (top left and bottom right), 120 (top), 121 (top), 129 (top), 137 (bottom left), 160 (top), 162 (top right and bottom right), 163 (bottom left), 165 (bottom), 170

Patrick Wiebe: Page 129 (bottom)

Wikimedia Commons: Page 151 (bottom)

Index

Meet Doreen G. Howard

Doreen G. Howard is one of the nation's leading experts in heirloom vegetables, herbs, and fruits. She has helped introduce heirloom varieties back into the garden and flavor back to our plates. She has spent a lifetime growing heirlooms, and she's serious about the flavors we're all missing.

Formerly the nationally acclaimed long-time garden editor at *Woman's Day* (from 1997 to 2002), and gardening columnist at *The Christian Science Monitor*, Doreen is also an author and photographer. She currently writes for *The Old Farmer's Almanac* and is fully involved in social media.

During two decades of gardening, Howard has grown over 300 varieties of vegetables and dozens of antique fruit cultivars. *The New York Times* featured Doreen and her edible garden in June 2008.

Howard is the author of many best-selling gardening and cooking books. Doreen won the Garden Association of America's highest honor, the Silver Trowel award, in 2010 for "Gardens that Heal." She won a 2009 Society of Professional Journalists award for "Microbe Management: How to Build Fertile Soil."

Howard lives in Roscoe, Illinois, with her husband surrounded by a one-acre garden packed with antique apples, berries, luscious heirloom vegetables, and unusual edibles such as amaranth grain and blue potatoes. This is her first book with Cool Springs Press.